Genius Next Door

Genius Next Door

Genius Next Door

A Generational Approach to Financial Health

Financial HEIRs Book Series

Dr. Paul T. Blake

www.FinancialHEIRs.com

Genius Next Door

Genius Next Door: A Generational Approach to Financial Health

Copyright © 2024 Financial HEIRs International, Paul T. Blake – All rights reserved

Under International Copyright Law, all rights reserved. No part of this book may be reproduced, stored in a retrieval system, or transmitted in any form, including by any means electronic, mechanical, photocopying, or otherwise in whole or in part without permission in writing from the author, except in the case of sermon preparation, reviews, or articles and brief quotations embodied in critical articles. The use of occasional page copying for personal or group study is permitted and encouraged. Permission will be granted upon request.

ISBN

E-book: 979-8-9920766-4-6
PaperBack: 979-8-9920766-5-3
Hard Cover: 979-8-9920766-6-0

Genius Next Door

Page Blank Intentionally

Table of Contents

PREFACE	1
CHAPTER 1 Juan Dough Learns Life's Recipe	11
CHAPTER 2 Pedro Goes to Washington	19
CHAPTER 3 Power of Three Generations	27
CHAPTER 4 Common Carl Plays the Lottery	36
CHAPTER 5 Glam Fasad's Compound Interest Awakening	43
CHAPTER 6 Crystal Merlot	50
CHAPTER 7 Wedding Bliss	58
CHAPTER 8 Dreams, Rhythms, and Motivation	65
CHAPTER 9 Financial Advisory Team	72
CHAPTER 10 Life Cycle Investing	80
CHAPTER 11 Epic Vacation	88
CHAPTER 12 Little Junior Arrives	95
CHAPTER 13 Family Education System	104
CHAPTER 14 Age of Responsibility	112
CHAPTER 15 Junior's Dream Job	121
CHAPTER 16 Increasing Life Spans	128

CHAPTER 17 Percent Giving Challenge	136
CHAPTER 18 Joy of Giving	145
CHAPTER 19 Wealth is Relative	152
CHAPTER 20 Junior's Free Money	161
CHAPTER 21 Genius Next Door	168
CHAPTER 22 Tiny House – Line of Credit	177
CHAPTER 23 Generational Wealth Transfer	184
CHAPTER 24 Financial Health is 90% Psychological	192
APPENDIX I Welcome to Financial HEIRs	200
APPENDIX II Everyday Ed	202
APPENDIX III Eduardo Magnifico	210
EPILOGUE	219
About the Author	221
BIBLIOGRAPHY	222

Note from the Author

Do you visit a doctor or dentist each year? Americans even visit their auto mechanic each year. Why not give the same attention to your family's financial health? Using the latest tips from the psychology of financial health, the Financial HEIRs Book Series will help each person in your family save up to $100,000. The *Genius Next Door* is about the lost art of saving money, improving your financial health, and implementing Dr. Blake's innovative idea to have young people *live off their investment interests.*

Follow Pedro as he immigrates to America, marries Crystal ... and they raise Junior.

Short, humorous, and inspirational stories merge Dr. Blake's innovations with the foundational principles during the past 50 years from numerous bestsellers like *Millionaire Next Door* (Stanley and Danko, 1996), *Rich Dad, Poor Dad* (Robert Kiyosaki, 1997), *The Money Book for the Young, Fabulous, and Broke* (Suze Orman, 2004), *Smart Money, Smart Kids* (Dave Ramsey and Rachel Cruze, 2014), and the often ignored *First National Bank of Dad* (David Owen, 2007).

The best discoveries in the field of behavioral economics are included, helping inspire financial health by using psychology to our advantage. Stories about Pedro's family also include ideas and principles from Nobel prize winner Richard Thaler, plus Morgan Housel and his bestseller *Psychology of Money* (2020).

Gen Z has responded favorably when learning about becoming an HEIR ... so why wait? This easy-to-read book has insights that anyone can understand and apply ...

regardless of your age or the age of your potential HEIRs. You will love the wholistic approach to generational financial health … and becoming the Genius Next Door!

Finally, there is plenty of space in the book to write down your thoughts. To use your time wisely, write down your thoughts as you go.

PREFACE

Congratulations! By picking up this book, you show a desire to improve your family's financial health!

Together, we can inspire each family member to save $100,000 to live out their dreams! Regardless of your age or theirs, what if everyone in the family is on track to save $100,000? If you already have $100,000 in savings, then what is next? Are your HEIRs on track?

If young people, whom we call HEIRs, moved out of the house with this type of discipline and financial head start, they could pursue their dream job and not worry about it only paying an average American salary. Even if a young person only gets halfway toward their goal of reaching $100,000 by a certain age, they still win. They spent their formative years learning patience, self-discipline, planning skills, and how to develop a dream and chase it!

The path to save up to $100,000 is not as challenging as it seems, as wages have increased. Additionally, legitimate opportunities now exist for young people to earn more than minimum wage. Financial HEIRs classes and consultations offer creative, socially acceptable solutions to help you and your HEIRs reach $100,000 or $120,000 by age 25. Our seventeen-year-old son is easily on track to reach $120,000 by age 25, and so are the younger kids.

One Family at a Time

Why do some families get ahead in life? How do some families start out poor yet end up quite successful? Change begins one person at a time … one family at a time.

We all agree that learning about money is far different than making solid financial decisions. Life is more complicated than just learning – or merely making money. We each make difficult choices about satisfaction, health, and a life lived to the fullest. How will you lead your family by example and train them toward financial health?

Perhaps you went into debt at some point and are now convinced to help your HEIRs avoid that mistake. Or maybe you were *house-poor* for years, barely able to afford to live because you had borrowed too much to get into a particular house. Each generation has a chance to break cycles and create new lifestyles.

The *Genius Next Door* is about the lost art of financial health and the art of inspiration to live this lifestyle. This book will provide you with ideas and opportunities to impact the next generation. After getting on track yourself, sowing into someone's life skills – instead of giving out money – is more effective in the long-term towards helping people break the cycle of poverty. You can establish a new norm for future generations!

HEIRs

Young people today have the opportunity to *live off their investment interests!* To become the *Genius Next Door*, why not have your kids benefit from compound interest? All it takes is an inspired parent or grandparent to guide them.

If a young person saves $120,000 by age 25 and invests that money at a reasonable rate of 7.5% until age 70, then they will have $3,000,000! Yes, that is correct … 3 MILLION DOLLARS. This $3,000,000 will be enough for them to live off their investment interest without dwindling their assets and have an average American income for that generation (as of 2023). The phrase "without dwindling their assets" is key, meaning they could live in this retirement season indefinitely and still have $3,000,000.

As for age-appropriate goals, ages 7-14 are largely for developing self-discipline. Next, when your HEIRs are ages 15-21, develop an effective model for your family. What is the overarching agreement per saving? What is the monthly process for allocating funds? Does their dream or plan need to be modified to stay motivated? Finally, the ages of 22-25 are the biggest years of actually saving money, so do not be surprised to see a young person save $80,000 of their $120,000 in those final few years. This means a young person with only $40,000 saved by age 21 is probably still on track.

If your HEIRs start between ages 7-14, they will never really know any different. You will be able to seamlessly merge them into this new lifestyle. By age 15, they typically want to earn a paycheck … so that they can spend all of it. But do not worry if you are starting in the 15-22 age bracket. Anybody who has a dream will surprise you.

What if their primary years of saving were from age 15-25? A ten-year period of inconvenience should be compared to the alternative … saving for 50 years from age 25-75. You might be shocked when you run the math as to which one is more fruitful. Also, it will be easier for a person to stay focused and motivated for 10 years than 50 years, and young people are much easier to inspire.

The essence of the message is that saving money should have near-term rewards, not just long-term rewards. By using the HEIRs method, adults play the part of ensuring that young people experience the near-term rewards. Instead of merely teaching young people to delay gratification, we can *reward* them for delaying gratification.

Did you know that kids love earning interest off their investments? They love getting *free money*, just like adults. Adults call it *earning interest*, a boring term that has failed to inspire Americans to benefit from investing. Perhaps we should change our style of motivation and give them a chance to experience the joy of free money … by letting them spend it or give it away!

One major key in this adventure will be positive peer pressure. At puberty, the brain switches toward valuing what "the group" thinks, even sometimes irrationally, as the brain is growing so rapidly. Young people will even make sacrificial choices … as they get joy from these relationships and value what their group thinks. Therefore, the question should be: Which groups will your HEIRs join? After reading this book, your family may want to join our Alumni Inner Circle (see Appendix III – Eduardo Magnifico).

Our kids and grandkids can become HEIRs as we guide them into financial health …

H	*Helpful and Generous*
E	*Educated Spender*
I	*Investor with Common Sense*
R	*Resilient Worker*

H.E.I.R.

Hard Work

We all had some jobs when we were kids, and I had more than most … a local paper route recycled our neighbors' cans and newspapers, sold grass seed (failed business), sold my grandpa's rock collection (one summer), sold vegetables from my other grandparents' garden (seasonal), shoveled snow, mowed yards, worked at a BBQ restaurant, worked at a garden center, and painted houses. This was all before I turned 18. And that does not count regular chores, deep cleaning our house, our checklist of projects on Saturdays, or hauling firewood to keep the wood-burning stove going (suburban experiment of the 1980s).

While we may not expect our kids to have this many jobs, it did not seem like I was overworked in any particular year while I was growing up. What I learned was to quit complaining. In hindsight, it was what I needed most, as it allowed me to think outside my own selfish desires.

Interestingly, I did not seem to have much money as a kid. We were only allowed to spend 30% of what we earned. Then we put 50% into savings, which went toward college, of course. Our charitable giving was 20%. My parents also had us pay for a few items to keep us from having too much cash for our age. So, in essence, it felt like I had just enough to get by.

After having conquered the mountain of complaining plus developed a solid work ethic, it seemed my success should have been in place. What was missing?

Dream

As a numbers guy, I was kind of amazed by the idea of compound interest. I recall hearing the classic story of a kid who started saving $200 a month at age 18 and had $1,000,000 when he retired.

Even though I heard about investing and compound interest as a kid, I never took advantage of it. It sounded nice, but I had no dream in place to inspire me to live such a lifestyle. My choices from age 22-25 reflected the lack of a dream to motivate a young person to stay on track.

What dream would inspire you to make some hard choices? Are we utilizing the power of dreaming to inspire our HEIRS to make hard choices?

Unstable Economy – Next 50 Years?

The next 50 years will be unstable, as we and our HEIRs try to recover from all the over-spending, especially by the American government, in the past 100 years. The past century has created a culture of debt. NASDAQ reported in 2022:

> "The global financial crisis of 2008 was supposed to have taught the world the dangers of excessive debt. But borrowing has shot up since then. The debt of governments, companies, and households was 195% of

global GDP in 2007, according to the International Monetary Fund. By the end of 2020, it had reached 256%."[1]

Unfortunately, in the 21st century, we have become worse at borrowing money!

In 2024, the Wall Street Journal noted that financial security, in general, feels barely achievable to most Americans.[2] Rising prices have put an enormous dent in American's finances. In 2014, which was ten years ago, half of Americans received some form of government assistance.[3] A similar statistic for 2024 is hard to find ... because it is alarming for our nation and tucked away from internet searches. The percentage has assuredly gone up.

How will you navigate the unstable economy?

The squeeze on the middle class is increasing, as a strong majority of middle-class Americans are now struggling financially,[4] not to mention the poor. Amongst the middle class who might have savings, their financial status is wobbling significantly. Do Americans have a twelve-month *emergency fund* saved up? For example, due to the unstable economy, you may lose your job or find another comparable job a year later. If so, a twelve-month emergency fund would be gobbled up by this scenario. An emergency fund could be held in various forms of

---

[1] See Dixon, 2022.
[2] "Financial security and a comfortable retirement were similarly labeled as essential or important by 96% and 95% of people, respectively, but rated as easy or somewhat easy to pull off by only 9% and 8% (Wolfe, 2024)."
[3] See Matthews, 2014.
[4] "Findings published by the National True Cost of Living Coalition show that 65% of Americans whose incomes are 200% above the national poverty line – which is about $62,300 for a family of four, often considered middle class – said they are struggling financially (see Henney, 2024)."

cash or investments as long as you could access the money in less than a week. Well, as of 2023, 80% of Americans have less than $50,000 saved,[5] assuming home equity is a separate discussion.[6] Since $60,000 is the average American salary, they would have spent their entire emergency fund if they lost their job for a year. They would run out of cash, even though they may have some equity in their home. Again, this is 80% of Americans, and we will call this *cash-poor*. Yes, it is an American definition of poor, but the state of the union is surprising.

The future does not seem rosy enough to turn the tide. In 2022, Bloomberg published an article entitled "Once-in-a-Generation Wealth Boom Ends for America's Middle Class."[7] The window is closing for the "easy jump up" in economic class, so a long-term and generational strategy is key. Nobody expects the next 50 years to be as calm as the previous 50 years. What will your family do?

Enter Pedro … the *Genius Next Door*.

Family Story

Join Pedro and his wife Crystal and their Junior – and some of their extended family – as they discover a simpler approach to money, hard work, generosity, and financial health. They stumble into the "psychology of money" and learn how to pursue their lives' different dreams. Junior ends up benefiting enormously from their generational wisdom, including from his grandparents Clark, Carl, Glam Merlot, and great-grandpa Pappy. As Pedro and Crystal walk through life, they have questions about their own financial health … not to mention how to raise Junior in the 21st century!

---

[5] See Flynn, 2023.
[6] Having equity in the home, partnered with little or no savings, is called being *house-rich*. This often occurs when people try to live the middle-class lifestyle when their income does not support it well. Being *house-rich* is not a good strategy, as it lacks diversification and is not flexible in emergencies. Owning a more affordable home – a smaller house, or a home in a different area – is much wiser than becoming *house-rich*.
[7] See Once-in-a-Generation Wealth Boom Ends for America's Middle Class, 2023.

FHI

Financial HEIRs International (FHI) is designed to help you with your personal finances. We offer classes and consultations to help you reach financial health. Your lifestyle ends up becoming a foundation upon which to build a generational inheritance.

We also help families with HEIRs. The focus is on how to help them dream, incentivize them, and then walk it out.

Together, we can break the crisis in America that perpetuates cycles of debt and financial errors … one family at a time.

To learn more, visit www.FinancialHeirs.com.

Before we begin the story about Pedro, Crystal, and Junior, it may be helpful to read a funny little diddy about John Doe … or Juan Dough.

CHAPTER 1
Juan Dough Learns Life's Recipe

Juan Dough had always known that money was important, but he was about to discover that it wasn't the be-all and end-all of financial health. Sitting at his kitchen table one morning, staring at a pile of bills that seemed to grew faster than his paycheck, he felt overwhelmed. A career change was on the horizon, as his job at the local bakery paid enough to make his budget as reliable as bread crumbs next to pigeons. Something had to change.

Juan had read somewhere that most people are not serious about financial health. They think about it sometimes, maybe after buying that second coffee of the day, but they don't really take action. The ones who are serious, though, are those with money left over at the end of the month. He saw online that "Saving $100,000 is simpler than you think!" So Juan was curious and determined to understand what separates the financial fit from the rest of us doughheads.

The first thing Juan realized was that he needed a dream. Not just any dream, but one that could drive him to get out of bed each morning with a purpose. "Your legacy is about to change!" he thought as he imagined his future. Maybe he would give away large amounts to charity, travel the world, or start a business. It was while pondering these dreams that Juan hit upon his own dream: he wanted to volunteer more time every year as his wealth increased. Inspired by the phrase Freedom and Flexibility,' Juan realized he could work less and help young people more often.

With his dream in place, Juan focused on financial behavior rather than just financial literacy. Numbers had never been his strong suit, and he figured it was easier to let the experts handle the complicated stuff while he focused on simple matters like earning more and spending less. After all, making money decisions could be more complex than baking a soufflé. "Time over Money," he mused, embracing the idea that his life did not have to revolve around dollars and cents.

He soon discovered that the secret ingredient to financial success wasn't just about cutting out the daily lattes or counting every penny. It was about small, consistent changes. Like bread baking slowly all day in a warm kitchen, Juan realized that making little adjustments could have a big impact. And speaking of dough, Juan couldn't help but chuckle at the irony that his last name was a synonym for money. It seemed like a sign that he was on the right track.

When he became distracted by the cares of this life, he refocused on his unique journey by reminding himself to think generationally and not compare himself to others who were one generation ahead.

Juan soon learned that monthly paychecks were a big motivator, as we enjoy seeing them increase. Likewise, no one likes seeing their monthly income shrink. Young people, he found, responded almost the same as adults when it came to their money. The time frame of a monthly "alert" was frequent enough to provide a short-term "reward or punishment," which was necessary to sustain joy or motivation.

"Financial health in only three hours a month" was a phrase that caught his attention, realizing that a little effort could go a long way in making sure his family was on track. In less than three hours a month, Juan had his entire family on track toward financial

Even the kids who thought budgeting was as exciting as watching yeast rise were suddenly engaged.

health. He had set a goal for each person in the family to save $100,000, and to his surprise, they were all motivated by their monthly paycheck of progress. Even the kids who thought budgeting was as exciting as watching yeast rise, were suddenly engaged. They all wanted to see their savings grow and investment interest increase, and they were willing to cut back on video game purchases and bubble tea runs to do it.

As the months went by, Juan noticed a change not just in his finances but in himself and his family. They were happier, more focused, and had even started volunteering together. His kids began to understand the value of money and time, learning that life was about more than just accumulating wealth.

Juan Dough had stumbled upon a recipe for success that involved more than just dough – both kinds. He realized that financial health was really about life, character, parenting, and joy. In the end, Juan didn't just learn how to manage money; he learned how to live a richer, more fulfilling life. As he sat down with his family one evening, watching them laugh and share stories over dinner, Juan felt a sense of peace. He had become a genius parent, raised well-rounded kids, and yes, he had beaten the system—not with money, but with love, wisdom, and a dash of humor.

Moral

Juan overcame the temptation to neglect his financial health. Once he discovered the secrets of motivation linked to dreams and an increasing monthly paycheck, he was inspired to spend less, save more, and enjoy watching his monthly investment interest grow each month. It felt almost like *free money*.

Evidence

In 2019, the *Journal of Financial Counseling and Planning* reported that happiness is linked to financial health.[8] This is different than saying that money leads to joy and happiness; rather, financial health does.

---

[8] "Even after accounting for participants' actual financial context, feelings of economic pressure, and relationship satisfaction, a positive association between sound financial management behavior and happiness remained." (Spuhler & Dew, 2019, p. 157).

Challenge

At Financial HEIRs, we inspire each member of the family to save $100,000 in order to live out their dreams! What are your thoughts on this goal?

Reflect

If you resonate with Juan Dough or his cousin John Doe, what would motivate you to make small changes in financial health?

What would help your HEIRs make small changes to their financial health?

While it is still fresh in your mind, what are the ideas you had while reading this chapter?

Genius Next Door

Write down an action item for this year ...

Now equipped as a true Juan Dough, you will be especially curious about how Pedro enjoys a big adventure on a trip to Washington, D.C.!

CHAPTER 2
Pedro Goes to Washington

Pedro was an ordinary man with common dreams and an unremarkable name. One day, he set out on the grand path of life, determined to make it to Washington, D.C., the land of influence, wealth, and power relationships. He was going to change the world. Along the way, Pedro was bound to face hurdles that would test his resolve. Thankfully, his greatest strength was his willingness to admit his flaws, even if he often overestimated how well he managed them.

Pedro's first hurdle on his path to D.C. was a tall signpost labeled "Stuck." He knew he had to keep moving, but sometimes, he stopped to rest by the roadside, staring at the clouds, and would think, "I'll get up soon." Days pass as Pedro sat there, waiting for a burst of motivation that never came.

Eventually, he decided to take action and jumped up with newfound energy. But this burst of enthusiasm had Pedro sprinting down the path like a man possessed. "I'm doing it! I'm really doing it!" he shouted. Unfortunately, he sprinted so fast that he tripped over a rock and tumbled off the path into a ditch. There he lay, face down in the mud, thinking, "Maybe I overestimated how to build this *hope* thing."

After dusting himself off, Pedro trudged on until he reached the second hurdle: "Fear of Change." Pedro stood there, shaking in his boots at the thought of change. "What if I don't like it? What if it's hard?" he mumbled, glancing nervously around. Trying to avoid the hurdle, he tiptoed around it, only to find himself on a narrow ledge above a steep ravine.

"That's it," he thought, "I'll just go back to the path!" But as he turned, he bumped into someone who handed him a note. It read, "You're not bad, Pedro, just physically uncoordinated." Pedro huffed, "That's not helpful!" He tried to throw the note away but tripped again, rolling down the hill into a puddle. "Well, pride comes before the fall, but at least I'm learning how to receive the truth," he grumbled, soaked but slightly wiser.

Pedro was willing to listen to the hard truth.

Next, Pedro came upon the third hurdle: "Contentment." On one side of the path, a carnival barker yelled, "Step right up! You'll never have enough unless you try your luck!" Pedro, ever curious, wandered over to see what all the fuss was about. Before he knew it, he was juggling ten different plans for getting rich quickly, none of which mentioned saving money ... not to mention hard work or common sense.

After losing his last dollar on a rigged game of chance, Pedro stumbled back to the path, grumbling about cheats and swindlers. He then noticed a serene meadow on the other side, where people sat under trees, enjoying simple pleasures like sandwiches and fresh air and insightful conversation. Pedro joined them, but after a few minutes, he grew bored of the quiet scene. "This is too simple," he muttered and wandered back to the carnival, realizing he was caught between greed and contentment.

Continuing on, Pedro faced the fourth hurdle: "Healthy Work Ethic." He set up camp on the side of the road and decided to take a little nap before tackling this one. When he woke up, he panicked, realizing he'd slept through an entire week. "I've got to make up for lost time!" he declared, working himself into a frenzy, trying to do everything at once.

Within a few hours, Pedro was exhausted, lying flat on his back again, mumbling, "Maybe I overestimated my stamina." He tried to pace himself after that, but it was a constant struggle between laziness and taking on too much.

Finally, Pedro reached the fifth hurdle: "Self-Control." He decided to have a snack to fuel up before attempting this one. But one snack led to another, and before long, Pedro had eaten his entire food supply. "I should have paced myself," he said, eyeing the empty bags and wrappers. Instead of growing in patience, he tried to sprint past the hurdle, where he stumbled and face-planted right before the finish line. Hey, even people without self-control can finish the easy route!

Sitting by the side of the path, Pedro realized that every stumble, every fall, every detour reflected his inner struggles. His path to Washington, D.C., was no different from his financial journey, which was disorganized due to his personal life. With a sigh, Pedro understood that until he got his act together, he'd keep tripping over these hurdles, whether on the financial path or the road of life.

And so, Common Pedro decided that maybe, just maybe, it was time to take a step back, reassess, and, perhaps, find a better map. Or at least learn to walk without falling over his own feet.

Moral

By improving our money decisions, we will make better non-financial decisions. By improving our non-financial decisions, we will improve our money decisions. They are all interwoven.

Evidence

"The same forces that shape our reality in the domain of money also influence how we value the important things in the rest of our lives: how we spend our time, manage our career, embrace other people, develop relationships, make ourselves happy, and ultimately, how we understand the world around us. ... Our decisions about money are about more than just money."[9]

"During interviews with old people in *30 Lessons for Living* by Karl Pillemer ... no one said to choose your job based on future earning potential. They valued quality friendships, being part of something bigger than yourself, and unstructured time with their kids/family."[10]

Challenge

"Life isn't any fun without a sense of *enough*. ... We will never become the richest person in the world. Instead, accept that what I have is *enough*."[11]

---

[9] See Ariely & Kreisler, 2018, p. x.
[10] See Housel, 2020, p. 89.
[11] See Housel, 2020, p. 41-42.

Reflect

Which sign most resonated with you and why?

Who could hold you accountable for a healthy work ethic?

While it is still fresh in your mind, what are the ideas you had while reading this chapter?

Genius Next Door

Write down an action item for this year ...

———

To better understand Pedro, you will want to meet his dad, Clark, and his grandpa, Pappy.

CHAPTER 3
Power of Three Generations

It may be helpful to hear about Pedro's family and upbringing to discover why he wanted to move to America and Washington.

Pedro was with his dad, Clark, and his Grandpa Pappy, sitting on the porch one sunny afternoon, each representing a different generation's approach to life. Pappy, a grizzled war veteran with a knack for telling stories, leaned back in his rocking chair, puffing on an imaginary pipe.

"You know, Pedro," Pappy began, "I fought in the war so your dad Clark could study something smart, like mathematics and philosophy." He waved his hand dramatically as if giving a speech to a crowd instead of two sleepy relatives.

Clark, an engineer with a love for numbers and a slight obsession with building model ships, chuckled. "And I studied all that to give Pedro here the chance to focus on the arts! Right, Pedro?"

Pedro, engrossed in balancing a spoon on his nose, looked up, cross-eyed. "Huh? Oh, yeah! I'm totally into poetry and... um, tap dancing?" He wasn't quite sure what Pappy and his dad were talking about, but he was pretty sure tap dancing would impress someone.

Pappy grinned. "See? We did our jobs right. Pedro, you get to study painting, poetry, music, or whatever tickles your fancy. Thanks to us, you have the freedom to choose."

Pedro nodded, although his thoughts were mostly just thinking about ice cream. "Sounds great! Can I study ice cream making as well?"

His dad, Clark, laughed. "Sure thing, Pedro. Freedom and flexibility are almost immeasurable. You can study whatever makes you happy."

Pedro beamed. "Awesome! I think I'll major in ice cream and minor in creativity. As long as I save most of my money, then it should work out fine." Pappy winked at Clark. "I think we've set him up for success. After all, 'How much we save is something we can control.' Now, how about we all study some ice cream together?"

And so, three generations bonded over scoops of vanilla and sprinkles, proving that, in the end, it's not just about what you study but who you share it with.

As they enjoyed their ice cream, Pedro thought about the power of three generations sitting together on that porch. Grandpa Pappy learned the value of hard work, adding that to Clark's family inheritance. Clark knew there was more to pass on than just a strong work ethic, so he realized the need for a broader understanding of financial health. Pappy was thrilled to see Clark adding to the family legacy.

Saving money is more important than our career choice.

With the freedom to pursue his passions, Pedro needed to be smart about saving money, wise about investing, and motivated to remain steady for many years. Clark wanted to give Pedro the wisdom to build a life of joy ... which included financial health.

Moral

Saving is something we can control.

About 100 years ago, there was a comic strip called *Keeping Up with the Joneses* by Arthur "Pop" Momand. In one comic, the judge declares to two married couples in his courtroom, "Well, well! It's the Joneses and their neighbors, who I see are still managing to keep up with them." Unfortunately, the judge was a bankruptcy judge. We may be *Keeping Up with the Joneses*, or we may just be wasting our time watching *Keeping Up with the Kardashians* ... a similar path toward bankruptcy. As I have decreased the time that is devoted to comparisons to those around me – as well as entertainment, while not eliminating it entirely – I have noticed a significant increase in life satisfaction.

An ancient proverb says it is destructive to be jealous of your neighbor's house or spouse. There is a powerful temptation to be greedy to obtain what we see around us. We are also tempted to compare ourselves to others. At what point will we start a new trend?

Our parents and grandparents hope we'll surpass what they've handed down to us. We could simply rely on their wisdom, but the best way to honor them is by building on the legacy they provided.

Evidence

Pedro did not feel the need to compare himself to his friends, his dad, or his grandpa. A key reason we cannot compare ourselves to others, whether neighbors or people from other generations, is largely because they have different goals, worries, and aspirations.[12] We also all have different gifts, as well as skills we have developed.

Where there is a will, there is a way to break out of generational cycles and create new ones. A famous American named John Adams, who was President actually, once said,

> "I must study politics and war, that our sons may have liberty to study mathematics and philosophy. Our sons ought to study mathematics and philosophy, geography, natural history and naval architecture, navigation, commerce, and agriculture in order to give their children a right to study painting, poetry, music, architecture, statuary, tapestry, and porcelain."[13]

---

[12] See Housel, 2020, p. 173.
[13] See Adams, 1780.

Adams had a vision for his life that included where his kids and grandkids would find satisfaction in their career choices.

The quote from John Adams resonates with many Americans like myself. My grandfather served in World War II, and then my dad studied business at Harvard. As a third generation, I find the subject of anthropology (universal traits) fascinating. What is universal? Specifically, how do humans of any age or culture relate to the subject of finances?

Challenge

We each build upon the legacy handed to us, so what are you building?

The "HEIRs lifestyle" results in your kids or grandkids becoming multi-millionaires when they retire at age 70 … because they will actually need that much to retire without government assistance.

Do you feel the power of three generations? Legacy! Done!

Reflect

What vision is your extended family pursuing?

What could you add to your family's generational inheritance?

What are a few monthly rewards for yourself that would inspire you to make small changes?

While it is still fresh in your mind, what are the ideas you had while reading this chapter?

Genius Next Door

Write down an action item for this year ...

Now that you know a bit about Pedro's dad, Clark, and his side of the family, you will be curious to meet Crystal's family!

CHAPTER 4
Common Carl Plays the Lottery

In order to best understand Pedro's wife Crystal and her upbringing, you should consider the path her dad, Common Carl, walked.

Carl Merlot was a man of simple pleasures, living in the heart of inner-city Chicago. Every week, like clockwork, he'd make his way down to the convenience store with $5 or $10 in his pocket, grab a lottery ticket, and spend the next few days dreaming of what life could be like if his numbers finally hit. Maybe he'd get himself a new car or take a vacation far away from the city to somewhere warm like Miami. Or maybe, just maybe, he'd buy a nice house outside the hustle and bustle of Chicago, where he'd never have to worry about money again.

For Carl, the real thrill wasn't in the winning—though he wouldn't mind that one bit—but it was in the anticipation. The hours leading up to the lottery draw were electric. He'd sit in his small apartment, staring at the ticket, imagining how his life might change in an instant. And when the numbers didn't match, which was usually the case, he'd just chuckle and say, "There's always next week."

Budgeting was not Common Carl's strength. The idea of tracking every penny sounded as fun as spending a summer afternoon on the overcrowded subway system. Once in a while, he'd tally up his yearly spending on lottery tickets – about $400 – and think, "That's just the price of dreaming big."

One hot afternoon, while hanging out with his friend Joe on their stoop, Joe hit him with a surprising thought. "Hey, Carl, what if you only spent $100 a year on lottery tickets and used the other $300 for a financial consultation? You know, with someone who could help you get ahead?"

Common Carl laughed. "A financial advisor? In my world? Come on, Joe, I don't need someone reminding me I'm broke. I already know!" But Joe wouldn't let it go.

"Think about it, Carl. Financial HEIRs International says, 'How much we save is something we can control.' Maybe it's time to take control of something, right?"

The idea rattled around in Carl's head for days. What if, instead of just dreaming, he could actually start building something real? Curiosity got the better of him, and he decided to give it a shot. He found a local consultant named Susan who worked out of a tiny office in the neighborhood.

Susan didn't promise him overnight riches, but she helped him see his money in a new way. She taught him how to set small goals and start saving, even just a little bit at a time.

Carl was hesitant to talk money with a friend, but he would listen to an expert.

Over the months, Carl noticed a change. He still bought weekly lottery tickets, now spending $5 instead of $10, and also built a growing savings account. His dreams of financial freedom were no longer tied solely to the luck of the draw—they were supported by his actions.

Maybe he'd never hit the jackpot, but Carl was okay with that. He wasn't just Common Carl anymore; he was becoming Carl with a plan, determined to take control of his future, one step at a time, in the heart of inner-city Chicago.

Moral

We spend more money than we realize.

We may want to keep playing in fantasy football leagues, raffles, or the lottery. However, we usually need to overcome a fear to become a better person. Or we may simply need to choose a priority that we already value.

Evidence

"The lowest income households in the U.S. on average spend over $400 a year on lottery tickets."[14] Other economic classes presumably spend far more on equivalent experiences.

Challenge

A financial consultation is within the grasp of most Americans, even when limitations of time and money are considered. As humans, we may fear big changes, but we do not mind making small changes. Which small changes are you ready to make?

---

[14] Housel, 2020, p. 18.

Reflect

Which of these two options makes the most sense? First, put $1,000 a year into savings. Second, use that same $1,000 a year to hire a financial consultant for $300 a year to help you advance your career and gain some key financial tips while still saving $700 a year.

Suppose you spend $40 a month on _____ (coffee, etc.). Would you be willing to spend $36 next month and $32 the month after that?

While it is still fresh in your mind, what are the ideas you had while reading this chapter?

Genius Next Door

Write down an action item for this year ...

If you thought Carl was a character, then meet Crystal's mom, Glam Fasad!

CHAPTER 5
Glam Fasad's Compound Interest Awakening

Glam Fasad, known for her love of extravagance, prided herself on appearances. She always drove the latest car, wore the flashiest clothes, and lived in a house that looked straight out of a magazine – complete with a mortgage that could make a banker blush. Glam's motto was simple: "Appearance opens new doors."

But one day, while flipping through a finance magazine in the dentist's waiting room, Glam stumbled upon an article about compound interest. Investments earn interest, but when your interest also earns more interest, this is called compound interest. The power of compound interest is legendary. The article quoted Albert Einstein as saying, "Compound interest is the eighth wonder of the world. He who understands it earns it ... he who doesn't ... pays it." Glam snorted. "Yeah, right," she thought. "If it's so wonderful, why doesn't it come with a Gucci label?"

Still, the idea nagged at her. After her dentist confirmed that flossing was non-negotiable, Glam started thinking about all the other things she'd been ignoring. She realized she'd heard about compound interest before – in math class when she was young – but she'd been too busy doodling in her notebook to pay attention. Now, at 32, she felt a twinge of regret for not starting sooner.

Around the same time, Glam noticed something else: the people she admired most weren't impressed by jewelry or expensive outfits. They cared about intellectual issues and spirituality, treating people with kindness, and making meaningful contributions to their communities. Glam realized her facade of wealth didn't impress anyone worth impressing.

As the façade was fading, and determined to reprioritize her life, Glam looked at her current financial health. She quickly learned that while she'd been busy keeping up appearances, her credit card debts had been compounding interest in the worst way.

"So, that's why I've been feeling poorer every month," she muttered, shaking her head.

Glam had never noticed that she was basically *paying* compound interest instead of earning compound interest. "Huh, I guess I will either *pay* a lot of interest during my lifetime or *earn* a lot of interest in my lifetime. It seems hard to walk the tightrope and do neither one."

Suddenly, Glam had a revelation. "I'm either winning astronomically or losing astronomically!"[15]

The average American now pays about $500,000 in interest during their lifetime.

Glam decided it was time for a change. She slowly paid off her debts and started saving, focusing on building real wealth through compound interest. As her savings grew, she found herself enjoying deeper conversations and building genuine friendships based on values, not vanity.

Laughing at her old self, Glam realized she didn't need a facade to feel wealthy – just the mystery of compound interest and a life focused on what truly mattered.

Moral

You do not have to be an Einstein to take advantage of compound interest, but you do have to save money. Eliminating debt harnesses the power of compound interest, but so does saving money. Are you winning astronomically or losing astronomically?

---

[15] Switch credit cards to a new company offering 0% interest for a few months. Then repeat! Never pay just the minimum on your credit card, as you will lose a ton of money. Also see Orman, 2005, p. 29-57.

Nobody budgets perfectly down to the penny. You are either erring on the side of the side of *over-spending*, or you are erring on the side of *over-saving*. Those are the only two human choices. If we fail to plan, we plan to fail.

What if we developed new interests or hobbies? What if we explored and discovered that we get more joy out of a new activity than our old weekly schedule? "You can spend less if you desire less. ... Most of what we get pleasure from – going for walks, reading, podcasts – costs little, so we rarely feel like we're missing out."[16]

Evidence

Half of Americans in 2023 could not pay off their credit card balance each month.[17] They are paying compound interest instead of earning it.

The majority of people alive today do not take advantage of compound interest. Why? They are human, and so we struggle to think beyond our immediate circumstances. In other words, we are not inspired to save money.

Challenge

Here's a pun for you ... If you have a lot of "change" or new ideas in your head, your family can call you head<u>quarters</u>. Seriously, as the headquarters of change in our family, do you want to develop a new path?

How do we incentivize a lifestyle that benefits from compound interest? Financial HEIRs have ingenious solutions to common problems within financial health. We emphasize generational health over immediate wealth, inspiring families to take advantage of compound interest *today*. We can live a life of hope, aim for the best, and serve those around us ... especially our HEIRs. How about Poverty to Philanthropy in One Generation?

---

[16] See Housel, 2020, p. 106, 216.
[17] See Herron, 2023.

Reflect

As a math genius, why was Einstein so fascinated by earning interest versus paying interest?

If you took on a new hobby, would you meet a new person? If you met the right person, would you be open to a new hobby?

While it is still fresh in your mind, what are the ideas you had while reading this chapter?

Write down an action item for this year ...

When little Crystal Merlot was born into Carl and Glam's life, she added a Grape Joy.

CHAPTER 6
Crystal Merlot

When Common Carl Merlot met Glam Fasad, it was love at first sight. They had some adjustments to make to pull off wedded bliss, but Carl's connection to Susan, the financial consultant, was quite helpful. Glam had recognized the power of compound interest, and they were curious about how to pull off this new life together. Before they knew it, a little bundle of joy named Crystal was born.

When Crystal Merlot moved out as an adult, she poured happiness by the glass ... just a swipe away on her platinum credit card. Her house was filled with the finest things money could buy – plush rugs so soft you could lose a sock in them, a high-tech espresso machine that required a PhD to operate, and, of course, an impressive wine collection that could rival a French cellar. Crystal loved her wine, especially merlot, not just because it shared her name but because it made her feel as sophisticated as a sommelier at a fancy vineyard.

Lately, Crystal has felt like her life was a bit like a cheap wine – overpriced and lacking in depth. So, one rainy Tuesday, while polishing her merlot glasses, she had an epiphany. She decided it was time to uncork a new way of living.

"First things first," Crystal declared to her cat, Pinot, who was her sounding board for all major life decisions. "I'm going to buy experiences, not things!" She booked a trip to a renowned vineyard in Tuscany, imagining herself swirling glasses of merlot with fellow wine enthusiasts. But when she arrived, she realized she'd forgotten to bring something crucial: friends. While everyone else was sharing stories and laughing, Crystal was swirling her glass alone, trying to look contemplative but mostly looking like she was sniffing the glass for mold.

"Clearly, wine tasting is a team sport," Crystal muttered to herself. "Or at least it's more fun when you're not the only one spitting into a bucket." So, she made a mental note to include friends in her next experience.

Back home, Crystal decided to buy herself sometime. "If time is money, then I'm buying it back!" she proclaimed, hiring a cleaning service and a gardener. On her first free Saturday, she poured herself a large glass of merlot and sat on her couch. "Ah, this is the life," she said, taking a sip. But soon, she got bored. "I can't just drink wine and do nothing," she thought, which was quite a revelation for someone with a wine rack in her living room.

To fill her time, she signed up for a wine-and-paint class, thinking it would be a delightful way to combine her love for merlot and the arts. However, after several glasses, Crystal's painting of a vineyard looked more like a Rorschach test than a landscape. "Well, they say art is subjective," she joked to her classmates, who were in stitches over her abstract masterpiece.

Crystal's newfound social life led her to host a potluck with a twist: everyone had to bring a wine that matched their personality. Crystal, of course, brought merlot. "It's smooth, full-bodied, and only gets better with age – just like me!" she quipped, winking at Pinot, who was busy batting at a cork.

By the end of the year, Crystal realized that her life was richer in ways she hadn't anticipated. She still had her merlot, but now it was shared over laughter with friends. She still bought nice things, but they were memories, not material items. And she still indulged herself – just occasionally, with a glass of wine and a side of generosity.

Research shows that experiences with loved ones bring greater long-term satisfaction than material items.

The holidays arrived, and Crystal decided to spend her money on others. Instead of expensive gadgets, she donated to a wine charity that provided vineyard experiences to communities in need. Her friends were delighted with the gesture, and one even joked, "You're the gift that keeps on giving, just like a good bottle of wine!"

Crystal Merlot had discovered the secret to happiness: experiences, time, and giving. And like a fine merlot, her happiness only grew deeper and richer with age. Cheers to that!

Moral

By focusing on experiences, saving time, and giving to others, people can maximize the happiness derived from their spending.

Evidence

In *Happy Money: The Science of Smarter Spending*, Elizabeth Dunn and Michael Norton explore how spending money can increase happiness by prioritizing experiences, time, and generosity. They argue that buying experiences, such as vacations or concerts, bring more joy than material possessions because experiences foster social connections and create lasting memories. Additionally, treating oneself occasionally rather than regularly indulging enhances appreciation and enjoyment due to the novelty and anticipation involved.

The authors also emphasize the value of buying time by outsourcing tasks one dislikes, such as cleaning or yard work. This allows individuals to focus on activities that bring joy, acknowledging that time is a finite resource. They highlight the power of anticipation, suggesting that paying for experiences upfront and enjoying them later can prolong happiness, as the excitement of looking forward to an event often surpasses the event itself.

Finally, Dunn and Norton present compelling evidence that spending money on others yields greater happiness than spending on oneself. Numerous studies show that acts of generosity, whether through gifts or charitable donations, foster social bonds and boost well-being.

Challenge

It can be hard to know what to give away, how much money to give, what to outsource, and what priorities are most important. On the other hand, if all our time is spent on experiences, we will not be able to give away or outsource.

Get organized! If you want a partner, find a financial consultant like Susan.

Reflect

What tangible items are not as valuable as you thought?

Genius Next Door

What experiences are more valuable than you realized?

While it is still fresh in your mind, what are the ideas you had while reading this chapter?

Write down an action item for this year ...

———

If you love weddings, then keep reading about how Pedro and Crystal pull off the big day!

CHAPTER 7
Wedding Bliss

When Pedro met Crystal, it just felt right. Her laugh was contagious, her smile magnetic. From that moment, he knew – this was the person he wanted to build his future with.

They had always known they were opposites in many ways, but it wasn't until they got engaged that they discovered just how differently they viewed money. For Pedro, money was like a safety net—save, save, save. It was more of a "live in the moment" thing for Crystal. Spend it when you've got it because who knows what tomorrow will bring?

The difference wasn't exactly subtle, and it started to become a source of stress in their relationship. One day, after a minor spat over whether or not they needed to spend $500 on wedding invitations, they realized they needed help. "We're going to have to talk about money more," Crystal said, sitting on the couch, scrolling through potential photographers.

Pedro sighed, his calculator in hand. "Talking, sure. But we need more than just talk. We need a plan."

That's when Crystal remembered something. "My dad, Carl, uses Susan for financial advice! Why don't we meet with her? She helped him with financial stuff beyond just numbers, and he's always singing her praises."

Pedro, who was always open to expert advice, nodded. "Alright, let's do it. But she better side with me on the wedding budget."

A week later, they were sitting in Susan's office, going over everything from flowers to photographers ... even the mini-chocolates at the reception. Susan, with her calm and methodical approach, helped them break down their wedding plans, making sure they saved on the high-ticket items in order to splurge on the low-ticket items. It felt reasonable but special. Pedro breathed a sigh of relief as they found ways to trim costs without sacrificing too much of the romance Crystal was keen on.

Once the wedding planning stress was under control, Susan brought up the bigger issue: their long-term financial health as a couple. "You both come from different financial backgrounds, but that doesn't mean you can't find common ground," Susan said. "The goal is to take what your parents handed down and build on it. You don't want to just freeload off their wisdom – you want to improve upon it."

Crystal nodded, liking the sound of that. "So, we make our own financial agreement?"

"Exactly," Susan smiled. "A legacy of your own."

Paying for weddings and children can be stressful, but why take that stress out on your spouse?

Of course, that's when Crystal dropped the bombshell: "I read somewhere that raising a kid costs $300,000 these days!"[18]

Pedro's eyes widened. "What?! That's more than we're spending on the wedding! What kind of plan would reach that lofty number!?"

Susan laughed. "You *could* wing it, but financial health isn't just year to year. You're building something lasting here. As we say at FHI, 'Invest in your legacy, not just your bank account.' It's not about constant worry, just consistent care."

Pedro and Crystal exchanged glances, realizing that their focus on romantic dinners and sunset walks would need to make room for a little planning. However, with Susan's unbiased input, they saw that their marriage would really benefit from an outside voice. Financial health could be tackled step by step – without

---

[18] See Parker, 2024.

losing the spark of their relationship. After all, love and money don't have to be at odds; and they just need a little balance.

Moral

Pedro and Crystal tacked on a challenging relational dynamic – aligning values. A third party like Susan helped relieve tension in those discussions and infused new ideas, like saving on high-ticket items in order to splurge on low-ticket items.

Evidence

"Money is the top reason for divorce."[19] What is a realistic response to this reality? Engaged or married couples should formulate a plan together, as aligning values takes time.

"Psychologists say that to learn from experience, we need frequent practice and immediate feedback."[20] Life often does not allow for frequent practice, so expert advice is key during those times.

Challenge

Pedro and Crystal should probably meet with Susan when they make big decisions that are infrequent – changing jobs, buying a home or a car, picking a college, wedding planning, etc. Perhaps they should meet with Susan quarterly for a year before moving to annual consultations.

---

[19] See Ariely & Kreisler, 2018, p. ix.
[20] See Thaler, 2015, p. 50.

Reflect

How have you handled stressful conversations about money with your relatives?

What advice would you give your HEIRs who are dating, engaged, or newly married?

While it is still fresh in your mind, what are the ideas you had while reading this chapter?

Genius Next Door

Write down an action item for this year ...

Next up ... Pedro is coming to America!

CHAPTER 8
Dreams, Rhythms, and Motivation

At age 25, Pedro set sail – well, flew actually – to the land of opportunity: America. He had saved diligently in his home country, which meant he arrived in the U.S. with more than hope and dreams – he also had a bit of money in his pocket. Pedro knew this was his chance to build a new life, and he was determined to make the most of it.

Soon after arriving, he found a job as a house painter for $25 an hour. Not exactly the glamorous career in ice cream he'd fantasized about, but $50,000 a year was far from a bad start. Sure, it was slightly below the American average of $60,000, but Pedro wasn't complaining. He saw it as a blessing – he was making more than he ever imagined. And the best part? He was just getting started.

However, Pedro quickly learned that saving money in America wasn't as easy as it seemed. Everywhere he turned, there were temptations: fancy gadgets, takeout, ads for things he didn't even know existed but suddenly desperately wanted. Every time he opened his wallet, it was begging for mercy. Pedro knew he had to stay disciplined, but that was easier said than done.

Fortunately, his wife, Crystal, had an idea. And not just any idea – a big, bold, somewhat crazy idea.

"Why don't we take a six-month vacation as a reward for saving?" Crystal suggested over dinner one evening.

Pedro stopped mid-bite, his fork hovering in the air. "A six-month vacation?" he repeated, raising an eyebrow. "Isn't that a little... ambitious?"

Crystal wasn't fazed. "Think about it! If we live simply now, we can save enough for the vacation of our dreams later. We could visit family overseas or take a long, relaxing cruise. It'll be both a motivation and a reward."

Pedro thought about it, and the more he considered the idea, the more it excited him. A six-month vacation—now that was a goal worth saving for! So, with that vision in mind, Pedro and Crystal committed to a disciplined lifestyle. They cut back on luxuries, stuck to a budget, and kept their eyes firmly on the prize: that epic vacation.

Pedro, being the planner that he was, didn't stop there. He decided to take a new approach to life. Instead of feeling bogged down by the grind of everyday work, he divided his life into manageable chunks: seven-year cycles. He figured that seven years was long enough to accomplish meaningful goals but short enough to avoid burnout. Inspired by an ancient proverb that reminded him life's challenges were temporary, Pedro felt empowered. He knew that no matter how tough things got, they wouldn't last forever.

Pedro dreamed about his six month vacation!

So Pedro added Crystal's suggestion to their seven-year plan: he would work diligently for six years, saving and investing like a responsible adult, and then take plenty of vacation days during the seventh year. It was the ultimate "work hard, play hard" philosophy, and Pedro was all in.

Moral
Pedro and Crystal found that a reward every 7th year could keep them motivated toward financial health each week.

Evidence
It is easy to lose motivation. By age 25, I was in the wrong house with the wrong car. Despite my upbringing, something went wrong with my financial decision-making.

Eleanor Roosevelt said, "The future belongs to those who believe in the beauty of their dreams."

Challenge
Crafting a dream that will keep you inspired may be simple, or it may take some time upfront, plus some polishing every year. Build a rhythm of "rest time" into our schedule once a week where you can pause and ponder.

Reflect

If seven-year cycles are unrealistic, what would work for you?

Genius Next Door

Why do great leaders "pause and ponder" each year?

While it is still fresh in your mind, what are the ideas you had while reading this chapter?

Write down an action item for this year ...

———

Next, you will see how Pedro avoided feeling overwhelmed as he built a team.

CHAPTER 9
Financial Advisory Team

With a dream in place, Pedro and Crystal set out to conquer the world. Yet their life in America had its complications. Pedro quickly realized that things like taxes, financial planning, and navigating a new culture were more complicated than they appeared. He needed help. A friend suggested that Pedro assemble an "advisory team" to help guide him through the financial maze.

Intrigued, Pedro took the advice seriously. They put together a small advisory team, which included Susan, the financial consultant (or as Crystal liked to call her, "the money whisperer") for $300 a year, an accountant for another $300 a year, and a trusted friend who was fluent in English. This way, nothing would get lost in translation, and Pedro could focus on what he did best: working hard and saving. They focused on staying in sync with one another relationally while the experts provided advice and services.

Susan was a lifesaver. She didn't just help with investments; she helped him with numerous aspects of their lives. Once a year, they'd meet for a full review, covering everything from budgeting and career advancement to personal obstacles and insurance needs. Crystal often joked that it was like therapy for their wallet, which worked wonders.

During one of their annual reviews, Susan uncovered a game-changing opportunity: free English classes in the evening. With improved language skills, Pedro could open doors to bigger and better career opportunities. "Why not take the classes?" she suggested. "They could lead to a promotion at your job."

Pedro liked the sound of that. So, he enrolled in the classes, and before long, his English skills improved significantly. This not only helped him communicate better but also positioned him for future success in his career.

Meanwhile, Pedro was determined to stick to his savings goal. He lived simply … sharing rides, having roommates, and making smart financial choices. He aimed to save $10,000 annually … 20% of his income. After four years, he had saved $40,000 and was now fluent in English. Not bad for someone who had spent only $2,400 on financial advice!

Pedro was living in the booming southern part of the U.S., where the housing market was growing faster than his English vocabulary. With so many new residents moving in, there was plenty of demand in the house painting industry. Soon, Pedro's boss needed a new supervisor, and with Pedro's four years of experience and improved English skills, he was the obvious choice.

The promotion came with a nice raise—an additional $10 per hour, bumping his salary up to $70,000 annually. For the first time, Pedro was making more than the average American.

Instead of splurging on fancy cars or designer clothes, they were focused on their dream of a six-month vacation! Susan encouraged them to save the additional $20,000 he was earning each year. In total, he was now saving $30,000 annually.

To prevent major lifestyle changes each month, Pedro simply saved the money he got from his raise!

After two years as a supervisor, combined with his previous four years as a house painter, Pedro had saved $100,000. Not bad for a guy who started with just a paintbrush and a dream! As his first seven-year cycle came to a close, Pedro was thankful for his advisory team and could feel a shift in his life. He had worked hard, saved smart, and was ready for the next big thing.

Moral

Did you know that the wealthy use a financial advisory team approach? Why? They recognize they will be better off. They realize they are more successful when they are held accountable by somebody, get financial tips from experts, and focus their energy where they have expertise. The wealthy are unashamed about using a financial advisory team. Consider using this comprehensive approach toward financial health.

Here is a mystery ... Where will you always find money? In a dictionary. The moral of this riddle is that being a good student will help you find money. Being willing to listen or learn will help you find money that you did not know you could access.

Evidence

The missing factor within the classic immigrant analogy is financial health, as the core values of hard work and education may or may not necessarily result in having any money left over ... at the end of the month or the end of their life.

A team approach will help protect us from ourselves ... our own ignorance, greed, fear, and weaknesses. We can lose a lot of money when we are the only brain involved. So, who is part of a financial advisory team?

1) Typically, a close confidant that you know well and trust (spouse, best friend, or partner) is the first person to consider.
2) Hiring an accountant is a great choice for many people. Accountants not only file taxes accurately, but they also help with questions about being an employee versus an entrepreneur.
3) A spiritual advisor (such as a pastor or a life coach) is helpful if you have personal obstacles in your life that are blocking you from being the best version of yourself. They will help you overcome life's temptations through prayer or

wisdom. Or, if you believe that supernatural forces might impact you or your finances, find help from somebody with spiritual expertise to help you win the game of life.
4) An advisory team would include a financial consultant like Susan, who helps educate you on options during an Annual Review. Financial HEIRs can function as your financial consultant.
5) An advisory team might include a Certified Financial Planner (CFP)[21] once you reach about $100,000, which is a typical minimum for CFPs to take on a new client. They will help you earn a good interest rate on your $100,000.[22]

Challenge

Nobel Prize-winning behavioral economist Richard Thaler popularized the idea that Americans prefer to save their upcoming raise as opposed to changing their lifestyle today.[23] Would you be willing to save all the money from your next raise?

---

[21] See Kagan, 2023. Or simply go to www.investopedia.com and search CFP. You will want to bookmark Investopedia, which provides enormous amounts of free information that has been verified by several professionals before being posted.

[22] A CFP is a financial advisor who invests your money, whereas your financial consultant is a financial educator and life coach. Considered adding a professional and licensed Certified Financial Planner (CFP) to your advisory team, not a local bank advisor who is limited to investment options which that bank sells. The CFP will help you decide where and how to invest. In a similar way that an accountant becomes a Certified Professional Accountant (CPA) [See Hayes, 2024. Or simply go to www.investopedia.com and search CPA.], a financial advisor becomes a professional CFP, handling investments instead of your taxes. CFPs work full-time using their financial expertise, licenses, and legal knowledge to help you get the best return on your money. CFPs handle the paperwork, bank transfers, and other transactions. They also produce the tax statements that your accountant demands. With $100,000 in a standard portfolio, you might average $5,000-$10,000 a year in interest. The CFP will charge an annual fee of roughly 1.5% of your portfolio ... or $1,500 if you have $100,000 invested. The fee will come out of the interest you earned, so it would not impact your monthly budget. Some people feel fee is worth it due to being able to sleep better at night knowing that a professional is handling their investments.

[23] Thaler, 2015, 314-319.

Reflect

Why would you or Pedro assemble a financial advisory team?

Who should be added to your financial advisory team?

While it is still fresh in your mind, what are the ideas you had while reading this chapter?

Write down an action item for this year ...

———

Pedro and Crystal are about to discover ways to invest if you do not have the free time or energy to make investing decisions.

CHAPTER 10
Life Cycle Investing

Before heading out for their epic vacation in year seven, Pedro and Crystal wanted to invest wisely to earn a better interest rate. After all, taking so much time off was a big loss in income!

Now, with $100,000 in savings, Pedro and Crystal found themselves in unfamiliar territory – too much money! They'd never had this much before, and suddenly, the stress kicked in. "What do we do with it?" Crystal asked, eyeing the savings account as it might explode. Should they stick with their dream of an extended vacation, or was that too indulgent? Should they buy a house instead? It was all a bit overwhelming. Pedro laughed nervously, "I thought having money was supposed to make life easier, not give us more decisions to make!" They quickly realized that managing success was its own challenge.

Most people would have rushed to buy a house, but their financial consultant, Susan, provided several options that Pedro and Crystal wanted to consider. Given the current economic conditions, they felt it was smarter to invest the money rather than put everything into real estate. The last thing Pedro wanted was to have all his eggs in one basket – especially a basket labeled "real estate bubble."

A brief internet search on buying a home versus renting a home will open your eyes to financial opportunities!

Pedro had always thought of the stock market as a mysterious maze full of animals like bulls and bears and something called a "short squeeze," which he suspected was either an investment strategy or an aggressive workout move. His strategy to avoid all that confusion had been simple: keep his money safely tucked away in a savings account, where it earned about as much interest as the change he found in his couch cushions.

One afternoon, during his annual financial review with his trusty consultant, Susan, Pedro confessed his hesitance about the stock market. "I just don't get it," he admitted, sipping his coffee. "It's like trying to understand advanced math while wearing a blindfold."

Susan chuckled, clearly used to hearing this. "Have you heard about Life Cycle ETFs?"

Pedro raised an eyebrow. "Life Cycle? Sounds like a setting on a dishwasher."

"Well, not quite," Susan smiled. "Life Cycle ETFs, or Exchange-Traded Funds,[24] are designed for people just like you – folks who want to invest in the stock market but don't want to overthink about it. These funds automatically adjust based on your age and your target retirement age."

Pedro leaned forward, intrigued. "So, you're telling me I don't have to check stock prices daily?"

"Exactly," Susan said. "Life Cycle ETFs start with a more aggressive mix of stocks when you're younger and slowly transition to safer bonds as you age. You can just set it and forget it. It's like having a personal financial manager who never takes a day off."

Pedro was sold. The idea of a smart investment that would adapt to his needs without him having to constantly monitor it was exactly what he'd been looking for. He decided to invest in a Life Cycle ETF geared toward his age group. "This is perfect," he thought. "Now I can focus on more important things, like finally learning to grill the perfect steak."

Two years passed, and Pedro checked in with Susan to see how his investments were doing. While his steak-grilling skills

---

[24] "ETFs offer low expense ratios and fewer broker commissions than buying the stocks individually ... so they are a cost-effective way to gain exposure to a broad basket of stocks with a limited budget" (Chen, 2024).

still needed some fine-tuning, his investments were going strong. The Life Cycle ETF had quietly and efficiently adjusted his portfolio, balancing risk and reward as the years crept closer to retirement.

Pedro realized he had found his ideal investment strategy: one that worked for him without demanding his constant attention. As he clinked glasses with Crystal over a celebratory dinner – complete with a slightly overcooked steak – Pedro toasted to his newfound financial peace of mind. Thanks to Susan's advice and his Life Cycle ETF, he could finally enjoy a stress-free investment journey.

Moral

The moral of Pedro's story is that investing doesn't have to be complicated. With Life Cycle ETFs, you can set a smart, automated strategy that adjusts gradually, just like you do. Life Cycle ETFs fit perfectly into Pedro's approach, letting him invest wisely without sacrificing his precious time.

Life Cycle ETFs are a type of exchange-traded fund that automatically adjusts its asset mix as you age. Early on, they invest in higher-risk stocks for growth. As retirement nears, they shift toward safer bonds, providing a simple, hands-off approach to long-term investing.

Pedro valued freedom, flexibility, and time above all else. He didn't want to spend hours each month managing his investments or stressing over the stock market. Instead, he preferred to focus his efforts on finding creative ways to save, change his career, increase his income, negotiate a raise, or pick up a side gig. Regarding financial health, Pedro believed that spending less and earning more were the keys to success.

Evidence

Classic investment advice would be for adults to be in a mix of stocks and bonds. But what mix should they be in? It depends on your age, risk tolerance, and goals.

ETFs are a very popular choice amongst investors nowadays, and Life Cycle ETFs are a type of ETF that adjusts automatically as you age.

Challenge

If vocabulary like "Life Cycle ETF" is scary, then Financial HEIRs is here to help.

Reflect

Who is a good candidate to consider the idea of investing in a Life Cycle ETF?

Genius Next Door

When did Pedro learn about Life Cycle ETFs?

While it is still fresh in your mind, what are the ideas you had while reading this chapter?

Genius Next Door

Write down an action item for this year ...

Pedro and Crystal are about to celebrate their seventh-year vacation!

CHAPTER 11
Epic Vacation

Vacation! Pedro and Crystal decided to take an extended vacation, not just any vacation ... a serious getaway. With Crystal by his side, they spent half the year traveling, visiting family overseas, or indulging in some well-deserved relaxation. They also enjoyed stay-cations at home, lounging around and reflecting on how far they'd come since he had first arrived in America.

Pedro was thankful for the extended break, as it took an entire week to get his body relaxed! But it wasn't until the end of the first month that he finally slowed down mentally.

It was during these moments of rest that Pedro had time to think deeply about his future. Most importantly, the vacation gave Pedro the chance to pause and ponder. He thought about the next seven-year cycle and what kind of person he wanted to become. He had made great strides financially, but he realized that life wasn't just about money. It was about balancing relationships, working hard, saving smart, and taking time to recharge.

After several months, Pedro realized he really *needed* rest. Ultimately, he decided to rest one day a week. No work ... and no working around the house either.

During these six months, Pedro ended up spending the entire $30,000 he had saved that year. But he didn't regret a single dollar. After all, what was the point of working so hard if you couldn't enjoy the fruits of your labor?

Pedro and Crystal took six months of vacation time in one year!

As Pedro geared up for his next seven years, he felt more motivated than ever. His advisory team helped him map out a plan for his next seven-year cycle. Pedro would continue saving $30,000 annually, with $10,000 set aside for big purchases and $20,000 for investments.

What about the $300 that Pedro paid his financial consultant and the $300 he paid his accountant each year? Worth every penny. The yearly consultations weren't just about numbers; they covered every aspect of Pedro's life. His advisory team had become his secret weapon, helping him make smart decisions, stay disciplined, and plan for the future. "Why change something that's working so well?" Pedro often thought to himself. With their guidance, he had built a life of stability and growth. As the first seven-year cycle wrapped up, Pedro was ready to embrace the next one.

With the help of his advisory team and his own determination, he had built a life that was not only financially successful but personally fulfilling. Who knew what the next seven years would bring? Pedro didn't have all the answers, but he knew one thing for sure: with a little hard work, a lot of discipline, and the occasional extended vacation, anything was possible.

Moral

Consider resting weekly and taking extended vacations every seven years. Seven-day weeks and seven-year cycles are examples of rhythms that help us with decision fatigue. When we feel overwhelmed with options or decisions, adding rhythms eliminates a lot of stress since we eliminate some of the needless choices. Rhythms also help us grow in patience.

Evidence

The University of Cambridge reports that extended rest periods are crucial for the body to physically slow down and the mind to gain clarity. Research shows that long-term rest clears toxins from the brain, enhances cognitive function, and boosts emotional resilience. Slow-wave sleep, particularly during non-

REM stages, plays a key role in this restoration, helping to process emotions and manage stress. Additionally, taking extended breaks from work significantly reduces stress, improves mood, and supports overall well-being by allowing both body and mind to recover from prolonged mental exertion.[25]

Research shows that getting into consistent rhythms or routines helps limit the number of choices we must make throughout the day. Rhythms, such as morning routines or predetermined schedules, conserve mental energy, allowing the brain to focus on more important decisions. This helps prevent "decision fatigue," which occurs when our brain becomes overwhelmed by too many decisions, leading to poorer judgment and stress. By establishing regular patterns, we free up cognitive resources, making decision-making more efficient and reducing mental strain. For example, waking up at the same time daily helps optimize energy levels and aid in better decision-making throughout the day.

Challenge

It may be hard to truly rest … no working from home, no chores around the house, no planned activities … just rest. Consider experimenting with new rhythms to discover the ones best for you.

---

[25] See IsHak, 2020.

Reflect

When is a good time for you to rest?

What is the benefit of weekly rest versus extended vacations?

While it is still fresh in your mind, what are the ideas you had while reading this chapter?

Genius Next Door

Write down an action item for this year ...

Pedro and Crystal are about to have a baby!

CHAPTER 12
Little Junior Arrives

At 32, Pedro felt like life was coming together. After seven years of living in America, he had saved $100,000, learned English, and even landed a promotion at his house painting job. But something was missing. Crystal was 29, full of energy, excitement, and big dreams … one of which included starting a family.

During the Annual Review with Susan, the newlyweds also tackled some of Pedro's personal spending habits. Apparently, Pedro had a soft spot for expensive snacks that, while delicious, weren't doing wonders for his wallet. Crystal, who was all about making the budget stretch further, continued with her job to help cover inflation and save toward her dream of having children. They also established a new dream, helping some family members move to America. It was a lofty goal, but they felt motivated to achieve it by the end of these seven years. Together, they had a new dream in place.

Well, plans change. Some of Pedro's family members were ready to immigrate to America, and being the family-oriented guy he was, Pedro couldn't turn them away. They used their $10,000 of big purchase money that year to help his family make the big move. It was a jolt to their plans, but life happens. In the big picture, it was a blessing as they began to focus on family. They realized that now may be the time to have children.

Year two of this seven-year cycle was wonderful, but they decided to hold off on the baby-making and focus on each other, enjoying their time together. "Why rush?" Pedro had said. "Let's just enjoy a year of quiet, no crying babies… unless it's me after losing at Monopoly." So, instead of spending their savings on cribs and diapers, they bought a second car for $10,000. Susan, their ever-reliable financial consultant, helped them choose the perfect car to serve them well into the baby years and beyond. It wasn't flashy, but it was reliable, and it got them where they needed to go. They also revisited their savings goals and giving plans, ensuring they were on track for the long haul.

By year three, Crystal's baby fever had kicked in, and before long, little Junior arrived. Pedro felt overwhelmed with joy – and, let's be honest, a bit of panic. Babies were expensive, as he quickly

---

Pedro realized that a baby meant they needed a bigger place!

---

learned. The $10,000 they had saved that year went straight to medical bills, baby furniture, and enough diapers to last a small army. Susan, being the financial genius she was, helped them plan for Junior's life. Pedro, who didn't have the privilege of learning financial health in his youth, was determined to give Junior a better start.

In year four, they made their biggest purchase yet – a small fixer-upper house. They eventually wanted several rooms in the house for more kids, so they had to pick the right fixer-upper. Due to their current income and assets, they could not use the "home buying via line of credit" strategy. So, with a $10,000 down payment, they got the keys to a charming little home that needed quite a bit of TLC. It wasn't much, but it was theirs. During the Annual Review with Susan, they analyzed the best neighborhoods, considered their long-term plans, and started talking about Pedro's next career move. He'd been thinking about launching his own house painting business, but the timing wasn't quite right.

Year five saw them diving headfirst into home renovations. They poured another $10,000 into fixing up their little house, making it more livable and comfortable for their growing family. Walls were painted (naturally, Pedro was a pro), floors were refinished, and they even installed new kitchen appliances that didn't look like relics from the 1980s. During their review with

Susan, they reassessed their insurance needs, and Crystal had one eye on expanding the family again. Pedro was beginning to feel that they would be able to afford this life in America.

As year six rolled around, another $10,000 went into home improvements. The house was finally starting to look less like a construction zone and more like a cozy family home. And during their Annual Review, Pedro and Susan had a heart-to-heart about his career. He realized he was motivated whenever he saw his paycheck grow, and that's when they both agreed: it was time to start his own business. Pedro's Masterpiece Painting was born.

By year seven, they were feeling the excitement of their dream coming true again. Junior finally had a baby sister. Instead of a cruise this time around in the seventh year, Pedro took a lot of time off work to help Crystal with the kids. It was an adjustment, but it was worth every moment. As Pedro rested and reflected, he found himself grateful for the opportunities he'd had over the last 14 years. From learning English to starting his own business, he was proof that America was the land of opportunity.

Now, at age 39, Pedro checked on his Life-Cycle ETF investment, which was now worth about $300,000! Wow! His commitment to saving over the years paid off! Thanks to saving $20,000 annually and earning interest between 5-10%, Pedro now earns roughly $20,000 a year in interest alone.

During their Annual Review with Susan, they worked through how much to save for retirement, how much could go toward quality-of-life expenses, and how much they could allocate to giving. They even started planning for Junior's future, thinking ahead to what it would take to raise a financially savvy kid – one who wouldn't just blow his money on candy bars.

After 14 years in America, Pedro marveled at his accomplishments. He'd gotten married, purchased and remodeled a small home, started his own business, helped family members immigrate, and still managed to take time off every seven years to rest and reflect. His only debt was a small mortgage on the house, and with each passing year, he felt more and more grateful for the opportunities America had provided.

Crystal, now 36, was eager to expand their family even more, as the new baby was so exciting! Junior, now 4 years old, was growing up fast alongside his baby sister, and Crystal's dream of having more children only strengthened. She wanted to be a mom with many kids, and with Pedro's business doing well, they felt more financially secure than ever before.

As they sat together on their porch one evening, watching Junior chase fireflies in the yard, Crystal turned to Pedro with a smile. "Do you think we'll ever have time for another big vacation?" she asked, half-teasing.

Pedro laughed, remembering their six-month paradise from years ago. "Definitely!" he said. "But let's make sure we're not using all of our 'big purchase' money on diapers first."

They both laughed, feeling content with the life they'd built and excited for what the future held. Whatever the next seven-year cycle brought, Pedro and Crystal knew they were ready to face it together – with a solid plan, a bit of humor, and, of course, help from Susan.

Moral

"Call it a clan, call it a network, call it a tribe, call it a family: Whatever you call it, whoever you are, you need one." -- Jane Howard

Evidence

Spending time with family is the most popular answer older people give when asked what they wished they had spent more time doing. This also requires that we somehow cultivate these relationships so that the time together is enjoyable instead of destructive.

Challenge
What do you need to "own" in order to salvage a broken or lost relationship?

Reflect

Instead of a vacation, who could you visit to give some extra attention right now?

What could you do to help the next generation?

While it is still fresh in your mind, what are the ideas you had while reading this chapter?

Write down an action item for this year ...

Crystal is about to explore the system of financial education that her kids will receive.

CHAPTER 13
Family Education System

Unfortunately, Pedro and Crystal did not have extra cash to start a savings account for Junior immediately, so they focused on improving their parenting strategies instead. "Start with the basics," Susan said. "Like teaching him that money doesn't grow on trees – neither do toys."

Crystal really liked exploring new parenting strategies. If they were going to expand their family, she needed to be smart. They also wanted to help somehow with the illegal alien crisis, maybe adopting some little ones. How would they train all these little munchkins?

Crystal had always wondered why no one seemed to talk about money until something went wrong. In her education, she learned about photosynthesis, quadratic equations, and how to write an essay on "The Great Gatsby," but no one taught her how to be self-disciplined enough to save for the future. Instead, financial literacy seemed like a mysterious skill passed down from parent to child – if you were lucky enough to have financially savvy parents. As Robert Kiyosaki put it, "Since we teach nothing about money in school, the ideas of money are handed down from parent to child for generations."[26] Crystal thought, "Great, so my financial future depends on whether my parents read *Rich Dad Poor Dad*?"

Determined to fill in the gaps, Crystal dove into the history of financial education. She found that after World War II, the Council for Economic Education was formed to equip students with the basics of economics and personal finances. "Well, that's nice," Crystal thought, "but judging by the number of people living paycheck to paycheck, that plan clearly didn't work out."

---

[26] See Kiyosaki & Lechter, 2001, p. 44.

The irony was that while schools focused on technical subjects like math and science – important, sure – almost everyone in America still struggled with money. Even those who took the one-semester high school finance elective (if they were lucky) still ended up with credit card debt, student loans, and car payments that made them question their life choices. Crystal couldn't help but laugh at the absurdity: we learn how to calculate the area of a triangle ... but never how to benefit from compound interest.

Curious about how other countries approached this, she looked into China's financial habits since they were known as aggressive savers.[27] In contrast to America's buy-now-pay-later culture, the average Chinese citizen saved over 20% of their income.[28] "Imagine saving 20% of your paycheck," she thought, imagining her friends' horrified reactions. "We better cut back on some of those monthly subscription services!"

Crystal discovered that saving a high percent is achievable!

The more Crystal learned, the more she realized the problem wasn't financial literacy – it was behavior. Knowing how to budget didn't stop people from impulse-buying that pair of shoes they didn't need or racking up debt for a weekend getaway. The real challenge was inspiring people to save, not just teaching them how to.

As she sipped her coffee, Crystal smiled and thought, "If the Chinese can save 20%, we can shoot for 21% and still drink good coffee ... just at home." It wasn't about becoming a finance expert – it was about finding that balance between enjoying life now and securing her future. And if she could inspire her friends to do the same, well, that would be a financial victory.

---

[27] See Chart of the Week: China's Thrift, and What to Do About It, 2018.
[28] See He, 2023.

Crystal recognized that the educational system was not going to train young people toward financial health. While young people may learn some financial talking points at school, she wanted her HEIRs to be inspired to make lifestyle choices. Crystal knew that education was a starting point, while implementation was done at home.

Moral

Crystal found herself learning about financial *behavior*, not just financial literacy. We have been through the current education system, and it is broken. Learning about money is different than being inspired to actually save money. Our youth are faced with increasing temptations toward laziness and addiction, making training even more challenging than a generation ago. We need an overhaul to the culture, and it begins with your HEIRs. We can offer our HEIRs a different education track.

My high school elective on "Economics" was about entrepreneurship and was quite interesting, and my siblings, uncles, and cousins are quite entrepreneurial. On the other hand, my high school elective class called Accounting was quite boring, and my college classes on Finance only trained you for a career in Finance. For anyone who wanted to go into the professional field of finance or investing, then these classes were quite relevant. Unfortunately, any materials that covered "personal finance" were brief and easy to learn, so why would teachers spend much time on that? Personal finance choices are primarily about psychology anyway, not necessarily finance. Presently, the educational system is not designed to teach our HEIRs financial *behavior*.

Evidence

Research shows that "brothers' incomes are more correlated than their height/weight."[29] The idea is that your kids will take on your financial traits more so than your physical traits!

---

[29] See Housel, 2020, p. 29.

In 2018, the *Journal of Family and Economic Issues* reported that millennials wish their family had more openly communicated with them about financial stewardship and even practical knowledge of personal finances.[30] Other academic studies show that "students demonstrated gratitude for helpful conversations and good examples from parents"[31] surrounding financial health. In summary, your kids and grandkids are hoping to learn about financial health, and they are thankful when they finally do learn about financial health.

Challenge

At Financial HEIRs, we offer classes and consultations because the educational system is failing. We believe family financial health starts with the adult, not the young person. Our goal is to help families build a culture of financial wisdom that inspires young people to reach financial health by age 25, not start at age 25. With basic yet ingenious tips, your HEIRs will be making wise, million-dollar decisions. Instead of learning finance late in life, they can stop saving by 25 if necessary and still enjoy a secure future.

---

[30] See LeBaron et al., 2018, p. 220-232.
[31] See Jorgensen et al, 2019, p. 553.

Reflect

Why did the Council of Economic Education fail?

Why did Crystal focus on financial behavior?

While it is still fresh in your mind, what are the ideas you had while reading this chapter?

Genius Next Door

Write down an action item for this year ...

Pedro is about to learn why age 25 really matters!

CHAPTER 14
Age of Responsibility

Crystal and Pedro were having a lively debate one evening about when a person should be considered financially mature. Why did Hispanic culture pick age 15 for girls' *quinceanera* celebrations of becoming a woman? Crystal, a deep thinker, believed that the brain plays a major role in when someone is ready to handle money wisely. Pedro, ever the practical one, pointed out his own experiences growing up and how life lessons hit him long before he even knew what the brain's "frontal cortex" was.

"You know," Crystal said, leaning in, "the brain isn't fully developed until 25. It is widely acknowledged in the medical world that the frontal lobe of the brain (pre-frontal cortex) is not fully developed until the mid-20s ... with 25 being the age usually emphasized.[32] We shouldn't expect financial responsibility from people until then."

Pedro raised an eyebrow. "Is that why car insurance gets cheaper after 25? Are we suddenly better drivers because our brains are smarter?"

"Well, actually, yes!" Crystal laughed. "The data shows people drive more responsibly after their brains finish cooking, so insurance companies give them a break. It's the same reason life and medical insurance cuts you off your parents' plan at 25 – they expect you to be grown up by then!"

It hit Pedro that this wasn't just about money; it was about responsibility. When he thought back to his life, he realized that while he had made some good decisions before he was 25, like working hard and saving to move to America, his true financial health didn't come until later.

---

[32] See Kersting, 2004, p. 80.

Pedro realized that even the American government acknowledges that young people might be "dependent" upon adults after 18, as American children can be claimed as dependent on their tax return after age 18 if they meet the "rules for dependency." "I thought I was doing well just taking care of the bills," he said, "but the truth is, it's the lessons I learned before 25 that helped me survive after 25."

Crystal nodded. "Exactly! This is why we shouldn't throw young people to the wolves at 18 and say, 'Good luck!' Their brains aren't ready for it, and the science backs it up. Financial planners even say not to give your HEIRs large sums of money before 25 because they aren't ready to handle it!"

Pedro chuckled, remembering his younger self. "So, when I was 18, and I thought I had it all figured out..."

"...You didn't!" Crystal finished, laughing.

Young people need financial mentoring from their family until at least age 25

They both agreed that an active mentoring relationship until age 25 was essential. Crystal pointed out how much time parents have to teach their children real financial wisdom, as key habits related to money form even before age 7, according to the University of Cambridge.[33] "If you start teaching kids about work,

---

[33] A study out of the University of Wisconsin showed that by age 3, children can grasp basic economic concepts such as value and exchange. See Holden et al., 2009. Even further, Taylor cited a 2013 study by Whitebread and Bingham who are from the University of Cambridge: "By about second grade or age 7, when we're still packing their school lunches and watching cartoons with them, our children have formed many of the thought processes that will impact their financial capabilities later in life as adults. A study from the University of Cambridge titled 'Habit Formation and Learning in Young Children' bears this out, explaining that many basic concepts relating broadly to later financial behaviors—things like budgeting, delayed gratification, and saving—will

money, and savings at 7, they'll be much more prepared by the time their brains are ready at 25," she said.

"Seven, huh? I was more focused on climbing trees," Pedro mused.

"Well, you turned out fine!" Crystal laughed. "But seriously, it's the perfect time to introduce financial health. Before age seven, they are learning to trust and follow instructions. Age 7 is when kids start getting interested in banks, shops, poverty, and work."[34]

While Junior was young, they realized that Junior needed to "experience the satisfaction of obedience."[35] Before exploring an abundance of choices, Junior needed to learn respect for the wisdom of the older generations. As Junior got older, they allowed him more freedom and choices.

As Pedro pondered the development of the brain, he struck up another conversation with Crystal. "If they get stubborn during the teenage years, you still have that final window of opportunity between 22 and 25 to cram those lessons in."[36]

"Exactly! Once they're on their own, they start realizing that maybe their parents aren't totally clueless," Crystal grinned. "So instead of throwing a Sweet 16 or 21st birthday bash, we should throw them a 'Financially Free 25' party!"

Pedro laughed. "I like it. A party for brains and bank accounts!"

In the end, they both agreed: while life can teach hard lessons early, true financial maturity comes with age … and good

---

typically be in place. The same University of Cambridge study goes on to explain that each child's development and learning is highly dependent upon the physical and social environment in which they live, noting that "children, being essentially social learners, acquire cultural practices effortlessly." See Taylor, 2022. Also see Whitebread and Bingham, 2013.

[34] See Berti and Bombi, 1988, p. 180-183.

[35] See Blue & Blue, 1992, p. 94.

[36] "Individuals' perceptions of their financial knowledge appear to drop after college as they enter the workforce. This may suggest a window of opportunity for financial counselors and advisors to help individuals as they begin their careers." See Tenney et al, 2021, p. 89.

guidance along the way. And as far as their own HEIRs were concerned, they had a solid plan to help them reach financial health by 25, and maybe, just maybe, throw a heck of a party to celebrate it.

Moral

An adult once asked a kid, "Why are kids so stubborn?" The kid replied, "I'm not going to tell you."

Seriously, while kids seem stubborn, they are less stubborn than adults. After age 25, our character, habits, and mindsets are much tougher to change. Most Americans' education is complete by age 25. There are exceptions to every rule, but frankly, most Americans' financial future is essentially determined by age 25.

Evidence

Our family follows this medical guidance when parenting at about age 25. Numerous times, we have told our HEIRs, "Your brain is not fully developed yet, so we are here to help." It is a scientific fact. This has been monumental in shaping how we have parented our children, and now our kids are open to the idea that they may not know or understand everything.

Our 18-year-old niece wants to be a stay-at-home mom instead of having a full-time career. After a one-hour meeting with her, she now has 12 goals for this year ... implementing one per month. Afterward, she will be on track to save $120,000 by age 25.

Challenge

With this evidence all around us, consider an active mentoring relationship with your kids and their financial health until age 25. An "active mentoring relationship" would be defined differently in each family. But it is not saying, "Well, you're 18 now, so you can decide." An ancient proverb says that a fool and his money soon part ways. If our HEIRs' brains are not fully developed, then they will probably soon part ways with their money due to immature decision-making. We have an obligation to help them, as they are not physically capable of thinking it through as far as we would want.

The Financial HEIRs process incorporates identifying a dream, the age of responsibility, and accountability. If you all have not saved up $100,000 yet, then it can be a fun family adventure together. It may take a family effort to accomplish this goal, but most goals worth accomplishing are not achieved alone.

Imagine one of your HEIRs at their next *coming-of-age* ceremony. You are watching one of them publicly demonstrate their maturity and abilities. It dawns on you … for their age. They are pretty savvy when it comes to financial health. Even if they do not pick a lucrative career, they are going to be just fine financially.

Reflect

Since scientists, government agencies, and businesses are aware that the brain is not fully developed until age 25, how should families respond?

With all of the celebrations we have for young people aged 13-21, how could those be modified to include a celebration of financial independence at age 25?

While it is still fresh in your mind, what are the ideas you had while reading this chapter?

Genius Next Door

Write down an action item for this year ...

———

Pedro and Crystal learn how to leverage Junior's childhood dreams into something beneficial.

CHAPTER 15
Junior's Dream Job

Junior's parents were on a mission to raise their son differently. They both agreed that the average American family does not train young people in financial health. They weren't about to let little Junior – affectionately known as Jun (hoon!) – become another statistic of laziness and wandering. His parents had been listening to financial experts like Dave Ramsey and Rachel Cruze, who often said things like, "We don't have a student loan crisis in America. We have a parenting crisis!"[37] That really struck a chord with them.

Determined to give Junior the best education society could offer, they started teaching him about money early. But instead of the usual allowance and piggy bank routine, they wanted him to truly understand the value of financial health. Their motto became, "As long as you save money, you can pick almost any job you want." It sounded simple, but to Junior, it was the key to unlocking his future dreams.

One day, Junior came home from school with big news. "Mom! Dad! I've decided I want to be a professional pogo stick jumper!"

His parents, always supportive, didn't bat an eye. "That sounds ... fun," his mom said. "Just remember, as long as you're saving money, you can do whatever you love!" And so, Junior began his pogo stick career, practicing every day after school.

Junior was inspired to save – to see his <u>spending money</u> increase!

---

[37] See Ramsey & Cruze, 2014, p. 160.

But more importantly, Junior saved almost every dollar he earned from odd jobs around the neighborhood, dreaming of becoming the world's best pogo stick athlete. To keep Junior motivated, Susan helped Pedro invent a system – customized to Pedro's family – where Junior would be able to spend the investment interest he earned!

Years later, Junior still loved pogo sticks – but more than that, he loved that he was financially secure. Sure, his friends laughed at his hobby of pogo-stick jumping, but Junior laughed all the way to the bank. After all, thanks to his parents' wisdom, he could now explore new career options *and* enjoy a secure future.

Moral

Junior did not pay much attention to his overall savings amount, but he definitely cared about how much interest he earned … since he was allowed to spend it.

Junior had been taught that his dreams were important alongside financial health, indeed intertwined with financial health.

A personal goal of mine is to honor my parents by helping their grandkids – my nieces and nephews – reach financial health by age 25. It is a great way to stay connected to each of them as they grow up. They do not have to become doctors and lawyers; instead, they get to pick the job of their choice.

Evidence

As the research on Gen Z is coming out, Dr. Jean M. Twenge noted in 2017 that Gen Z values individualism, safety, and financial success. They value making money at their job more than finding it emotionally satisfying (as compared to Millennials and maybe also Gen X).[38]

In 2020, the *Journal of Financial Counseling and Planning* reported that healthy financial parenting led to increased GPAs for

---

[38] See Twenge, 2017.

young people.[39] This is a very interesting discovery! Even if their dream is to jump on a pogo stick, as adults, we can focus on their financial health, which will help them get better grades!

Challenge

Our role is to inspire our HEIRs toward a career they will enjoy, plus equip them to thrive economically right now. Saving $100,000 is simpler than you think!

---

[39] "Explicit financial socialization seemed to contravene such troublesome academic–financial behaviors such as worrying about finances, contemplating dropping out (unenrolling) before completing a college degree and failing to remain concentrated on academics. These concerns were associated with poorer student GPA, whereas the social influence of a parent for financial decisions made a positive contribution to student GPA" (Sabri et al, 2020, p. 277-278).

Reflect

Why was Junior motivated to take odd jobs when he wanted to jump and play all day?

Junior had unrealistic dreams, but how did his parents steer those dreams toward something beneficial in the long run?

While it is still fresh in your mind, what are the ideas you had while reading this chapter?

Write down an action item for this year ...

Pedro is about to learn that he may be alive for a really long time!

CHAPTER 16
Increasing Life Spans

A spry Boomer grandparent, Pedro's dad, Clark, retired in 2020 at the age of 75 and is now happily making plans to live well into his 90s. After all, thanks to advances in diet, exercise, medical care, and even natural remedies, why not? He has more energy than his own dad, Pappy, at 65.

As Clark and Pedro sit on the porch together, Pedro looks at his dad and thinks, "That could be me!" But there's a catch – Pedro doesn't plan to slow down just yet.

Pedro, now clearly in the mid-life season, is coming to terms with the reality of 21st-century retirement. Gone are the days when people clocked out at 65, collected a pension, and coasted into their twilight years. "Retire at 65 and die at 75? That's 20th-century thinking," he jokes. In this century, with people living longer, healthier lives, Pedro sees himself working until at least 75. The idea of keeping a part-time job, gradually easing into fewer hours as his body slows down, seems like the perfect way to avoid retirement woes. Who needs to retire when you can still enjoy a steady paycheck and keep your thumbprint on all the action?

As part of Gen Z and born in 2010, Junior dreamed of living to see the year 2100, which sent Clark and Pedro's minds into a tailspin. "We're raising 22nd-century kids!" they exclaimed. That means Junior could potentially be working and living well beyond what Pop and Pedro ever imagined.

Junior spent some of his formative years wondering why his parents and grandparents didn't do more to save and plan. He had some burning questions about society, his own financial scenario, and life in general. "Why did everyone print money until inflation made us poor? Why didn't the schools teach financial health? Were we really prepared to live to 100, or did we just hope for the best?" Junior had valid questions as Pedro chuckled under the tension. The truth is, Junior's concerns were real.

With life expectancy pushing 100, Junior must save for a retirement that could last 30 years or more – from age 70 to 100!

Clark's dad, Pappy, started saving after World War II, and Clark did the same since it worked well for his dad. Pedro followed the same pattern, as saving early, like around age 25, is

---

Junior earned interest for 80+ years like Warren Buffett

---

just common sense. As they began to talk, though, they both agreed that the key for Junior would be to start at age 10 or 15.

Clark had seen a newspaper article that week mentioned Harwood's renowned book on intergenerational communication,[40] who had pointed out, "It is very difficult to retire at 55 and retain a high quality of life for perhaps 30 or more years."[41] Clark realized that for most Americans, saving enough money to last for three decades of retirement is nearly impossible. Clark and Pedro are hopeful that with the right inspiration and a little nudge, Junior won't be living paycheck to paycheck in his golden years.

Clark, ever the wise patriarch, taught Pedro the importance of starting young. And now Pedro was improving that wisdom for Junior: "Start saving before age 25, or you'll end up scrambling later. Living longer is only an advantage if you start preparing early. Otherwise, it's just a long stretch of wondering how you'll pay the bills."

Instead, thanks to Clark and Pedro's example, Junior might just end up financially savvy enough to live well into the 22nd century – retired, relaxed, and wondering why everyone didn't start around age 10-15 like Warren Buffett.

---

[40] See Worthington et al., 2018.
[41] See Harwood, 2007, p. 273.

Moral

If we live into our 90s and 100s, the government cannot afford to pay for millions of people's retirement. Anyone trusting the government to pay for 30 years of retirement is placing their trust in the wrong hands!

You are training your HEIRs to have the character and the financial abilities to carry numerous roles. One of those roles will be to carry *you* in your final decade when you really need it. As we age, we will want our HEIRs to help us.

Evidence

As a healthy middle-aged male, my doctor and financial advisor told me to plan to live to age 95, so they must be reading the same data.[42] We plan accordingly.

Additionally, we tend to live longer if we are financially healthy. In 2022, the *Journal of Family and Economic Issues* addressed a link between finances and physical health, reporting that when our HEIRs can improve their finances, they will have better physical health.[43] This may seem surprising, but it seems true given that financial struggles cause stress, which is a leading cause of health problems.

Warren Buffett is famous for having earned 22% annually on his investments over 40 years, which is way above average. However, other investors, such as Jim Simons, earned 66%. The key is that Buffett invested for a longer period of time, developing an interest in investing at age 10.[44] Now age 94 (in 2024), Buffett has earned billions in the past few years, and 99% of Warren Buffett's net worth was accumulated after he was 65 years old due

---

[42] In 2019, the American government's Centers for Disease Control website reported that Americans aged 75 were expected to live another 10-15 years, depending on ethnicity and gender (National Center for Health Statistics, 2019).
[43] "The combination of financial literacy (ability to act) and financial access (opportunity to act) has a positive and longitudinal effect on health" (Sun & Chun, 2022, p. 744).
[44] See Housel, 2020, p. 61.

to compound interest.[45] If you are saving money, then it's quite possible that most of the money you make will be later in life.

Challenge

The 20th century is over, and we learned a lot. Perhaps the most important thing we learned in the 20th century is that the 21st century will be very different. Technology has changed almost everything, including how long we will live. We are looking to anthropology – what is universal to humanity – to navigate through these rapid changes and stabilize how we engage with a high-tech world.

In order to beat the system, why not have your HEIRs start saving at age 10-15 instead of 25? Many people have heard this idea, yet few have responded. We need a team-family approach and the motivation to stay disciplined. Therefore, the true question is one about inspiration, not knowledge. Humans also need relationships or a community to establish "who we are" and implement a culture of positive peer pressure. Financial HEIRs is here to help you develop an achievable plan for your entire family … a plan that inspires people to actually save some money.

Young people have an opportunity to follow in their path, starting at age 10 and investing until age 95-100. You can beat the system the old-fashioned way! Instead of barely surviving from age 70-100, our HEIRs could be running the country.

---

[45] See Konish, 2024.

Reflect

How will increasing life spans impact your financial health?

How will increasing life spans impact your HEIRs' financial health?

While it is still fresh in your mind, what are the ideas you had while reading this chapter?

Genius Next Door

Write down an action item for this year ...

———

Next up ... Pedro and Crystal look at giving an increased percentage of their income.

CHAPTER 17
Percent Giving Challenge

Pedro had always been a practical man. He worked hard, saved diligently, and made smart financial decisions. But when it came to giving away money, he found himself in unfamiliar territory. Now that he had some financial success in America, Pedro realized he had more than enough. In fact, he had *plenty*. And when you have plenty, people start to notice.

One Saturday morning, as Pedro sipped his coffee, Crystal walked in, reading from her phone. "Pedro, I think we need to talk about giving." Junior asked why we didn't help 'the nice man from the email' who needed money to save his kingdom".

Pedro almost spit out his coffee. "A Nigerian prince again?" he asked, shaking his head. "Does Junior really think we can save the world one fake prince at a time?"

Crystal smiled, but there was a serious point behind the joke. "We need to teach Junior about generosity, Pedro. But more than that, we need to figure out how to be smart with our giving. There's a fine line between helping and falling into a scam."

Pedro sighed, realizing she was right. He'd been avoiding this conversation for a while. As his business grew and their savings account blossomed, more people started coming to him with requests for donations. It wasn't that Pedro didn't want to help—he did. But how much was too much? And how did he figure out who truly needed help and who just saw him as a walking ATM?

Crystal's well-reasoned arguments about increasing their family's generosity never quite hit home with Pedro. Every time she brought up the idea of giving more, Pedro would nod politely, but in the back of his mind, he was already calculating how many more houses they'd have to paint to make up for the lost income. "I get it, Crystal, I really do," Pedro would say, "but you know, paint doesn't buy itself." It wasn't that Pedro was stingy; he just had a hard time imagining their money going off into the unknown, especially when the unknown didn't come with a warranty. But then, one evening, as Crystal presented another thoughtful case for giving, Pedro interrupted her mid-sentence. "Wait, where exactly is this money going?" he asked, genuinely curious for the first time.

Crystal, sensing an opportunity, quickly pulled up a website for a local cause that helped struggling families in their community. They both spent hours researching, reading success stories, and imagining the impact they could have. For the first time, it clicked for Pedro. Giving wasn't just about the numbers— it was about real people, real change. "All right, let's do it," he finally said with a grin. "But let's just make sure it's a real cause … something better than Junior's 'help the prince' strategy!" Crystal laughed, knowing that this time, Pedro's heart was finally in it.

"Why don't we start small? We don't have to give away huge sums right away. We could increase our giving by just 1% every year," she said.

Pedro squinted. "Like a slow-motion Mt. Everest?"

"Exactly," Crystal laughed. "We can increase our generosity, but in a way that's achievable and doesn't feel like we're risking the farm. Last year, we gave away 10% of our income. Let's aim for 11% this year."

Pedro liked the idea. It was practical but challenging enough to push them out of their comfort zone. And it wasn't like they didn't want to give – they just wanted to do it wisely. A key to their new giving strategy was that it basically put a limit on their giving, as they heard too many stories about people unwisely

---

Giving away a percent of our income keeps our budget steady. When a pay raise comes next year, then we can give more.

---

giving away too much of their money.

They sat Junior down that evening to explain their plan. "Look, buddy," Pedro said, "we're going to be generous, but we have to be smart about it. Not everyone who asks for money really needs it."

Junior frowned. "But what about the Nigerian prince?"

"Let's stick to real people for now," Pedro said with a smile. "People we can see and help directly."

Over the next few months, Pedro and Crystal made their giving plan more concrete. They vetted charities, researched causes they believed in, and set up a family budget for donations.

To their surprise, as they gave more, their opportunities seemed to grow. Pedro got a couple of new painting contracts, Crystal found a freelance gig she loved, and even Junior got a tip when helping the neighbors with yard work. It felt like they were being rewarded for their efforts.

One night, as Pedro tucked Junior into bed, Junior asked, "Dad, does giving make us rich?"

Pedro chuckled. "Not rich in money, son, but rich in life. Being generous helps us share what we have, and it feels good to know we're helping others. Plus, it's a lot better than helping imaginary princes."

Junior smiled, satisfied with the answer, and Pedro closed the door with a feeling of contentment. Being generous, he realized, wasn't just about giving money. It was about giving thoughtfully, sharing wisely, and, most importantly, teaching Junior that true wealth came not from what they kept but from what they gave away.

Moral

An ancient tale tells the story of a widow giving away her last coin. The lowly woman gave a high percentage of her money; in fact, she gave all. The story teaches that giving a high *dollar amount* is not as big of a sacrifice as giving a high *percentage*.

We all want to live more generously and inspire our HEIRs to be generous and escape the trap of selfishness. Why? Intuitively, we know that selfishness is a trap. Financial generosity is one form of combatting this selfishness.

Evidence

If you have $100 and give a quarter to charity, do you have $75 or $99.75? In America, unfortunately, the answer is that, in essence, we would have $99.75.

Based on the percentage of Americans who now give away, we have become selfish people. Americans give about 1.5% to 2% of their income to charity. This is regardless of whether they are rich or poor, as the rich and the poor give about the same percentage.[46] As a country, we have all fallen into the trap of selfishness. It is embarrassing that we Americans only give away two percent of our income!

In the 1800s, a now famous man named Hudson Taylor had a goal of living in China one day. To achieve this goal, he decided to live off one-third of his earnings so that he could develop self-discipline for such a lifestyle switch and culture shock. What did he do with the other two-thirds of the money that he kept earning? He gave it away. The standard of living in the 1800s was far inferior to the 2020s, yet he made the choice anyway. Hudson Taylor gave away a high percentage of his income.

Dale Losch tells the story of his family's success in increasing their giving percentage almost every year of their marriage.[47] Imagine that! Our family has a similar story ... navigating the challenges of increasing our giving percentage each year.

---

[46] See Priday, 2020.
[47] See Losch, 2020, p. 7-8.

Challenge

How much money is enough? "Try to stop moving the goalpost of *enough*."[48]

When it comes to an annual budget for your family, maybe setting a limit would be wise. Do you want to live off the average American salary? Or maybe you prefer to live off the average salary in your zip code? Setting a budget limit is a great way to say "NO" to the endless pursuit of more. A budget limit functions as a stopping point, and unless the budget says there is a stopping point, then we do not tend to stop.

One way to incorporate a budget limit is to set a goal to save a certain percentage of your income and give a certain percentage of your income. This is an investment into your future, your HEIRs' future, and other families' futures. After establishing your savings and giving percentages, take those out of your income first. The rest is what you will live off.

Our HEIRs are watching us and often imitating us.

---
[48] See Housel, 2020, p. 216.

Reflect

What would inspire you to give away a higher percentage of your income?

What is a realistic plan for your HEIRs' generosity track?

While it is still fresh in your mind, what are the ideas you had while reading this chapter?

Genius Next Door

Write down an action item for this year ...

―――――

Next up ... Pedro's entire family learns how to maintain joy when giving.

CHAPTER 18
Joy of Giving

Pedro and Crystal had a mission: to teach Junior about the joy of giving. Sure, Junior was a bright kid, but as a rapidly growing boy at age 14, he mostly found joy in food, candy, and games, not giving it away. But Pedro and Crystal were determined to show him that giving is actually more fun than buying yet another fast-food meal.

One Saturday afternoon, after Junior had just blown through his money at the store, Pedro sat him down for a chat. "Junior," Pedro began, "have you ever thought about giving your money away instead of spending it?"

Junior looked at his dad like he had just suggested they stop having pizza for dinner. "Why would I do that? Then I wouldn't have any money for fun!"

Crystal chimed in. "Well, it's not about having less. It's about feeling more. Do you know how excited you get when you get something new? Giving can make you feel like that, too."

Junior scrunched up his face, skeptical. "But giving away $1 doesn't sound fun. That's enough for a candy bar."

Pedro laughed. "You're right! Giving away $1 might not feel that exciting. But imagine giving away $20 or $50! The bigger the gift, the bigger the joy."

Giving away more money than usual is a key to JOY

Crystal nodded in agreement. "It's the same excitement you get when buying something you want. Except this time, you're helping someone else. It's like this, Junior. After a while, giving away $1 feels normal. But the joy comes back when you step it up and give $20."

Junior was starting to come around. He liked the idea of doing something that made him feel good. "So, if I give away more than I used to, it'll be more fun?"

Pedro grinned. "Exactly. And that's why we're going to start giving a little more each year. We're going to bump up our giving by a percentage."

Junior's eyes widened. "Wait, how much are we giving now?"

"We should have you start out by giving away 10% of your money," Crystal said. "But next year, we're going to raise it to 11%."

"Whoa," Junior said, clearly impressed. "That's a lot of money. But can I give it wherever I want?"

Pedro and Crystal exchanged proud glances. Their plan was working. "That's the spirit!" Pedro said. "How about we start talking about good ideas for people in need?"

Junior thought for a moment, then nodded. "Okay, but if I'm giving away more, does that mean I can still have pizza for dinner?"

Crystal laughed. "Deal. But the joy of giving might make you feel fuller than the pizza."

As they all high-fived, Junior realized something: giving wasn't just about losing money. It was about feeling joy excitement, and making a difference. His selfish lifestyle did not add up when he considered how the rest of the world lives, so maybe he would try to increase his giving each year. And who knew? Maybe, just maybe, giving could be even more fun than eating.

Moral

Young people naturally think about themselves. HEIRs have learned that giving is more fun than receiving. Giving to family members, friends, or the needy is more fun than receiving a gift, but we only know this through experience. We can give our HEIRs the experience of giving.

Financial health includes the joy of giving. But sometimes, we get so busy trying to divide the pie equally that we forget that with a little courage, we could simply bake another pie. Next year, we could give away more pie if we simply bake another pie! Our opportunities to earn more and give more are right around the corner if we simply live courageously today.

Evidence

Citing various academic studies, Hyatt summarized that generosity makes us healthier and happier, lowers our stress, improves our relationships, and extends our lives.[49] All these studies confirm the ancient proverb that says that he who sows generously will reap generously. We will reap a reward if we sow into other people's lives.

Challenge

Ask your HEIRs if they could live off 10% of their income. You may be surprised.

---

[49] See Hyatt, 2024.

Reflect

What would inspire you to give away a higher percentage of your income?

Genius Next Door

What is a realistic plan for your HEIRs generosity track?

While it is still fresh in your mind, what are the ideas you had while reading this chapter?

Genius Next Door

Write down an action item for this year ...

Junior is now set to tackle the challenging subjects of greed, fear, death, and taxes ... with Pedro's help.

CHAPTER 19
Wealth is Relative

Pedro sat down with Junior at the kitchen table one Saturday afternoon, determined to have "the talk." No, not *that* talk, but the one about wealth. Pedro had a favorite saying: "Wealth is relative." And for him, it was doubly true. Not only was he far more financially successful than his parents, but his wealth was also largely *because* of his relatives. Family meant everything to Pedro and Crystal, and they were determined to ensure their parents were cared for as they aged. And, of course, Pedro was considering an inheritance for his kids.

But getting Junior to care about long-term financial planning at age 15 was like trying to get him to voluntarily clean his room. Pedro knew he had to get creative.

One evening, Pedro sat down with Junior and tried a different approach. "Son," he began, "you've heard the phrase 'nothing is certain but death and taxes,' right?"

Junior looked up from his phone, mildly interested. "Yeah, I guess."

"Well, I'm going to switch it up for you," Pedro said with a grin. "Think of it as 'nothing is certain but health and wealth.' The idea is that physical health and financial wealth impact everyone, plus every society ... just like death and taxes."

Junior raised an eyebrow. "Health and wealth, huh?"

Pedro nodded. "Yep. Both are personal and societal concerns. And I'll tell you something I learned from Ron Swanson."

"Who's that?" Junior asked, looking suspicious.

"An eccentric fictional character," Pedro said with a serious tone. "Ron once said, 'I'm not sure how much money I have, but I do know how many pounds of money I have.'"

Junior snorted. "Pounds?"

"Exactly," Pedro laughed. "Sometimes it's more important to have money than to obsess over counting it. Health and wealth are relative. If the people around you seem healthier or wealthier, you might feel you're missing out. But that's just comparison talking."

Junior thought for a moment. "So, I should focus on having money, not counting it?"

Pedro grinned. "That's a good start. And remember, true wealth isn't just about having money – it's about having enough to help others, too."

Junior smiled and concluded, "It seems that wealth is all the stuff I didn't buy."[50] Pedro knew his lesson had hit home.

Suddenly, Junior's eyes shifted into a panic. "But what if we invest it and lose it all?" Already, his health was at risk due to his fear of wealth.

Pedro realized he needed to teach Junior about the irrational fear of losing all your wealth due to market crashes. Junior had started earning some money from a part-time job and had been showing interest in investing. However, he was also developing a fear of the dreaded "economic crash" he'd heard so much about.

Losing money in a market crash is FAR better than being broke!

"Junior," Pedro began, leaning back in his chair, "I know you're a bit nervous about investing your money because you're scared of losing it all in some big, scary crash. This is partially because you are doing a good job connecting your hard work to your wealth."

Junior nodded, eyes wide with concern. "Yeah, I've been reading online. Some people lost a lot of money in those crashes."

Pedro grinned. "True, but put this into perspective ... say you've saved up $100,000 ..."

---

[50] See Housel, 2020, p. 98.

Junior's jaw dropped. "$100,000? Dad, I'm still working for minimum wage!"

Pedro chuckled. "I know, but you may be surprised how quickly it adds up since you save almost all of it. So you've saved up $100,000, and then a market crash hits. Historically, crashes drop the market by 20 to 30 percent. So, instead of panicking, you'd look at your statement and realize you still have $70,000 to $80,000."

Junior's eyes narrowed. "Okay, but what if it's worse than that? What if it's like one of those *huge* crashes?"

Pedro nodded sagely. "Good question! Let's assume it's basically the worst crash in American history … so disastrous it doubles the typical crash. You'd still be left with $50,000."

Junior frowned. "But that's still losing half!"

Pedro leaned forward, eyes twinkling. "Ah, but remember our key: wealth is relative. After such a crash, with $50,000 in hand, you'd be wealthier than *almost everyone* in America. Most people won't have that kind of money because they didn't save or invest at all! And guess what? The people who thrive in post-crash economies are the ones who have money left to invest in new opportunities. You'd be in an amazing position."

Junior looked thoughtful. "So… even if I lose half, I'm still better off than most people?"

"Exactly!" Pedro exclaimed. "And that's the liberating part. The fear of losing wealth is irrational when you realize that you're still going to be better off than most. Like you, people who save and invest will always have more opportunities after a crash because they've prepared during the good times through hard work and saving."

Junior cracked a smile. "Okay, that makes sense. But what about people who don't save?"

Pedro shook his head. "Those people will struggle. They won't have any cash to take advantage of the post-crash economy, and worse, they didn't spend the good years learning how to be disciplined with their money." After pausing a moment to let it sink in, Pedro concluded by saying, "I'm going to save up *enough* money, and so should you. Wealth is relative. And our relatives will be relatively healthy and wealthy ... despite the circumstances."

Junior grinned, the lightbulb finally clicking. "Okay, Dad. I'll start saving. I mean, I'd rather have cash after a crash than be the guy saying, 'I should've listened to my dad.'"

Pedro chuckled, patting him on the back. "Exactly! Stick with the plan, and when the world's in chaos, we'll be the ones sitting pretty – relatively healthy, relatively wealthy, and ready to help our relatives."

Moral

Fear of saving and investing is irrational. The idea to "spend it all now in case we die early" ... well, this mentality is the opposite of helping the next generation and has led Americans into financial distress.

Evidence

Wealth is not only relative to our neighbors around us, but it also originates with our *relatives*. Whether through genetics or learned traits – nature versus nurture – our health and wealth are shaped by family.

In 2018, the *Journal of Financial Counseling and Planning* addressed how "improved financial literacy may contribute to improved self-esteem and increased psychological, physical, and emotional well-being."[51] As you learn about financial health, you will feel more empowered. Now, we are getting to the root of some issues.

---

[51] See LeBaron et al, 2018, p. 268.

Challenge

Financial HEIRs can help you get on track to a new career, a new budget, and a new lifestyle of self-discipline. Now is the time to change your monthly schedule. It is *relatively* easy. Imagine how many generations will benefit from this health and wealth.

Reflect

What areas of greed or fear in your life need addressing?

What areas of excess entertainment in your life need to be addressed?

While it is still fresh in your mind, what are the ideas you had while reading this chapter?

Write down an action item for this year ...

Junior is about to learn more about investment interest and Free Money!

CHAPTER 20
Junior's Free Money

Junior never passed up free money, so when Pedro and Clark came to him with a deal, he can't resist. The goal? Save $120,000 by the time he turned 25. But here was where Pedro and Clark came into the story. For every $100 Junior managed to save, both Pop and Pedro would give him $10 to spend. That meant $20 in free cash every time Junior hit the century mark. To a young person, it was like winning the lottery.

The only hitch was that Junior could not spend his $100. He could only spend his free money … the $20. It was like living off his investment interest, and he was inspired to save.

Junior's mind raced with the possibilities. "So, you're telling me, if I save $1,000, I get an extra $200 just like that?" he asked, eyes wide with excitement. Pedro chuckled. "Exactly. You save, and we'll reward you for being smart with your money."

That was all Junior needed to hear. Suddenly, saving money seemed like a game, and he was determined to win. Every dollar he earned from chores, birthdays, and even selling old toys was carefully tucked away. He even started cutting back on his candy and video game purchases. After all, he didn't want to miss out on those extra gifts from Grandpa Clark and Pedro. "Why spend $10 on candy," he'd think, "when I could save it and turn it into $12?"

As Junior grew older, the stakes got higher, but so did his motivation. Between the ages of 10 and 25, Clark and Pedro made little deals and adjustments to keep things interesting. Sometimes, Pedro would pay investment interest on the large amount of

---

There are numerous affordable ways to incentivize your HEIRs

---

savings that Junior was accumulating. It was a surprise bonus!

Other times, when Junior called Clark with a monthly update, Clark would double up his offer. Junior felt like he was pulling one over on the system each time, outsmarting the world and turning savings into a cash-boosting machine.

By the time Junior was 18, while most of his friends were blowing their part-time job money on food and gadgets, Junior was laser-focused. Thanks to Pedro and Clark's contributions, he knew that every dollar he saved was growing and that his future self would thank him. He began thinking strategically, even investing a bit here and there with Pedro's guidance.

At 25, Junior reached his goal with a grin that stretched ear to ear. Not only had he hit the $120,000 mark, but he had exceeded it, reaching a grand total of $125,000. "I really beat the system!" he said, triumphantly holding up his savings statement.

Pedro and Clark, proud as could be, just shook their heads. "You sure did, Junior. You've got the system figured out better than most adults." Junior smirked, feeling like a financial genius.

Not only had Junior saved a substantial amount of money, but he also learned the power of discipline and delayed gratification, watched his savings grow, and experienced the joy of giving. Perhaps best of all, he had a lifetime of financial lessons under his belt – all thanks to a little insightful motivation from Pedro and Clark.

Moral

Junior learned that free money exists in the form of family members giving to him regularly. However, the free money did not stop there, as Junior earned interest from his investments, which was another form of free money from businesses. Pedro and Clark could teach him about risk and investing later at an age-appropriate time. Instead of being discouraged that money does not grow on trees, Junior had a different view ... people who save get all sorts of bonuses in life, like free money.

Evidence

Research shows that unpredictable rewards are particularly effective at capturing and maintaining our attention. This is because they operate on what psychologists call a "variable ratio schedule." In this reward structure, the timing or frequency of rewards is unpredictable, which leads to a release of dopamine – the brain's reward chemical – especially when the reward is uncertain. The thrill of not knowing when the next win or reward will come keeps people interested in the activity. This principle can be applied in healthy ways, such as using surprise bonuses or rewards to motivate people in learning or workplace settings. When applied responsibly, this method can boost engagement and motivation.[52]

Challenge

If you need more help creating a Free Money system that works for your family, then Financial HEIRs has more ideas for you to consider. Whether how to afford a Free Money system, what to do with Junior's money, or how to keep Junior inspired ... we can help your family stay on track.

---

[52] See Weinschenk, 2013.

Reflect

If Junior lives off his investment interest, would he be the smartest kid on the block?

List some of Junior's options if he continued saving until age 25.

While it is still fresh in your mind, what are the ideas you had while reading this chapter?

Write down an action item for this year ...

In the next chapter, Pedro and Crystal become the Geniuses Next Door!

CHAPTER 21
Genius Next Door

As Americans interested in financial health, Pedro and Crystal had numerous questions about how to pass along a legacy of financial health to their son, Junior. The basics of checking accounts and credit cards were rather simple. Even still, Junior found these topics to be boring.

They were looking for something that would reach Junior at his age level, along with being inspirational toward Junior wanting to change his life choices. Even though children of immigrants are likely to get ahead compared to most American kids,[53] Pedro and Crystal wanted to ensure Junior got over the hump. Pedro realized his immigration to America helped inspire him toward financial health, but what would inspire someone like Junior, who had been raised in America?

Pedro decided to strike up a conversation with his financial consultant at Financial HEIRs at his next Annual Review. Pedro realized that he delayed having kids until his 30s, saving up a large amount of money after age 25 by living very frugally. What if Junior ended up making different decisions as an adult? It forced Pedro to consider that saving money before age 25 would have made a big difference. Perhaps Junior would be able to take advantage of the land of opportunity at an earlier age! But how would Pedro inspire Junior to actually take action, given the temptations that come within a culture where our needs are often met?

There were plenty of new ideas for Pedro to consider. Financial HEIRs' short video classes on "Free Money" helped them catch a vision for how to inspire Junior to live off investment interest. Financial HEIRs' short video classes on "Family Bank" helped them understand how to afford financial incentives that

---

[53] See Abramitzky & Boustan, 2022.

would inspire Junior along the way. Financial HEIRs' short video classes on "Million Dollar Decisions" were enormously helpful for Junior, as Pedro and Crystal were thrilled to see Junior getting a dream and vision in place for his life.

Crystal also noticed that leaving a legacy was appealing to grandparents. Since the short video classes at Financial HEIRS were "universal" and relevant for any age, gender, or culture, she decided to include her parents, Carl and Glam, in this education process from start to finish. Due to their years of wisdom, they would appreciate this approach to financial health. Their insight on the value of time and their free time to help their grandkids launched them into the process wholeheartedly. In fact, since Crystal had two sisters with kids of their own, Carl and Glam had numerous grandkids and recognized the value was bigger than just helping Junior.

Carl and Glam only talked about money once a month with the grandkids. This guideline helped them build a family culture that was not focused on money but rather a periodic emphasis on financial health. Pedro spent less than three hours a month working toward this goal of helping Junior's financial health, which counted Pedro's time watching a video, helping Junior track spending, or periodically inspiring Junior to continue living off his investment interest.

Pedro and Crystal had made sacrifices related to quality of life in order to help the next generation. Surprisingly, Junior did not have to make nearly as many sacrifices because he started earning interest much earlier than Pedro. Pedro was concerned that Junior would never stick with the plan. He was pleasantly relieved to see that Junior did not have to make enormous sacrifices that would

---

You may be surprised at how easily your HEIRs merge into this lifestyle

---

truly bother a young person … other than the universal need to learn a healthy work ethic!

Ultimately, Pedro and the extended family decided to join Financial HEIRs' Alumni Inner Circle to connect with other families trying to walk in financial health. They benefited from interacting with other families, getting creative ideas, and hearing stories of perseverance. Occasionally, they were able to share a lesson their family had learned in this whole adventure. Ultimately, one of their main objectives was to help their HEIRs make some friends who were also beating the system, as it helped Junior and his cousins see that there were other economic geniuses his age. Secretly, Crystal wondered if Junior would someday marry one of these other economic geniuses they met through the Alumni Inner Circle.

Moral

Pedro and Crystal were the Geniuses Next Door.

After examining the cultural idea of *what is cool* in America, it became clear to Pedro that to be cool in America, a person should break the trends. It does not matter if the trends are healthy or unhealthy. As long as one breaks the trends, then many people will consider you cool.

Unfortunately, this is a horrible trend in society. Pedro recognized that wisdom was not being applied when deciding which cultural norms should be preserved versus challenged. Pedro saw that society was now paying the price for such a bankrupt definition of *cool*.

At the same time, Pedro decided to be cool by breaking the trend toward debt. He also wanted Junior to be cool, so their family decided to break the trend of financial irresponsibility.

Millionaires and immigrants alike have taken a similar path toward financial health.

Evidence

When Junior turned 25, he had a college degree, no college debt, and had saved $120,000. While this seems unachievable today, an inspired young person will find this goal very achievable. Junior could use this as his retirement since it would turn into $3,000,000 by age 70. You read that correctly ... 3 million dollars! Or he could go to graduate school, start a business, or spend the interest each year toward an increased quality of life. Due to Junior's large savings, his financial consultant at Financial HEIRs helped him follow in his parent's footsteps by hiring a CFP and a CPA.

Challenge

At Financial HEIRs, we can help your entire family. Our innovative and generational approach helps adults get on track, along with inspiring their HEIRs to live off their investment interests. Most adults started experiencing the joy of earning interest around age 25-55, but the next generation can start much earlier!

If you and your HEIRs are looking to invest before saving $100,000, we can also explain options for that. We have developed a "no hype" way to beat the system. You can easily join this Generational, Generous, and Genius approach to living life.

Reflect

True or False: Pedro was constantly trying to teach Junior about money.

Why did Junior feel cool?

Genius Next Door

What is a Genius Next Door?

While it is still fresh in your mind, what are the ideas you had while reading this chapter?

Write down an action item for this year ...

———

Next up, Junior buys a house ... in genius fashion!

CHAPTER 22
Tiny House – Line of Credit

At 25, Junior decided it was time to finally move out of his parents' house. His parents had given him the speech … "It's time for you to spread your wings." But he knew this moment was coming, as they had talked a lot about "age 25." Plus, with $125,000 in savings, he figured he was ready. He might not know everything about adulting, but he knew it was better than explaining to a date why he still lived in his childhood bedroom.

Junior met with Susan, the financial consultant, on his own, and she mentioned using a "line of credit" to buy his first house. It didn't really land in his long-term memory; he was just glad to be moving out. None of his friends talked like Susan did, so he marched forward with his grand scheme to finally move out of the house.

Junior was ready for the big moment at the bank: his first house. Mortgages and loans sounded confusing, but he had one goal – don't sound clueless. "I just want to buy a house," he told the banker, trying to look serious.

The banker leaned in and said, "You know, since you have $125,000 in investments here, you don't need to worry about a traditional mortgage or paying closing costs."

Junior blinked. "No closing costs? What's the catch?"

"No catch," the banker said. "You can use a line of credit instead. You borrow $50,000, pay for the house, and just pay us the interest. No monthly payments on the principal itself for five years. And when five years are up, you can either pay off the $50,000 or just borrow the $50,000 again."

Junior scratched his head. He wasn't sure what a line of credit really was, but he was pretty sure he liked the idea of not paying about $2,000 in closing costs on a $50,000 mortgage. His mind briefly wandered to the pizza rolls he could buy with the money he'd saved. The banker mentioned something about Loan-to-

Value ratios, but Junior was already imagining himself in his own place – no roommates, no mom yelling to clean his room. Bliss.

"So, I could buy a house without all the extra mortgage stuff and just pay $208 a month?" Junior asked.

"Exactly," the banker said. "You're living the dream. You'll be living smart while your friends are shelling out big bucks for rent."

No closing costs PLUS low rent is a no brainer

That was all Junior needed to hear. He signed up and soon moved into his $50,000 tiny house, as a friend let him park it on their property. Sure, the house was barely bigger than his parents' garage, but it was his. He grinned as he sat on his porch (which doubled as his entire front yard). His friends were stuck paying rent while he was living the good life as a financial genius.

As he sipped his coffee, feeling like the king of his tiny castle, he remembered something he'd seen on the Financial HEIRs website: "Freedom and Flexibility ... Time over Money." He chuckled. "I guess I'm figuring out what financial health really means."

Moral

There are rare scenarios when borrowing makes sense, but not paying closing costs on a home is one of those occasions worth considering.

Evidence

The option to buy a home on a line of credit is just the beginning of options your HEIRs will consider once they have money. There are numerous benefits to having saved up your money, many of which are not discovered until you find yourself in the situation.

For a line of credit secured by investment assets, banks often use a Loan-to-Value (LTV) ratio. A common LTV ratio for investment accounts ranges from 30-50%. This means if your investment account is valued at $100,000, you might be eligible for a line of credit ranging from $30,000-$50,000, depending on the bank's policies and the quality of your assets. The ratio can also vary based on your credit, but banks give lower interest rates to people who have money. At a 5% rate, Junior's $50,000 loan meant a tiny house loan payment of only $208 a month.

Challenge

Shopping for tiny houses helps young people get an idea of how realistic it could be to live simply. Family outing?

Reflect

Due to the increasing cost of living, what living arrangements make economic sense in the 21st century?

Genius Next Door

How could you help your HEIRs find quality roommates?

While it is still fresh in your mind, what are the ideas you had while reading this chapter?

Genius Next Door

Write down an action item for this year ...

―――――

Stay tuned as Pedro and Junior develop a plan for Junior's kids ... and their neighbors!

CHAPTER 23
Generational Wealth Transfer

Pedro never aimed to be a financial mastermind. He wasn't born into wealth and didn't dream of becoming a prince or elite billionaire. His goals were simple: raise a family, give generously, live comfortably, and pass on enough wisdom (and maybe some cash) to his kids.

In his recent annual review with Susan, she mentioned "generational wealth transfer." She told him that according to experts, most kids who receive an inheritance of money lose it all by the second or third generation. Pedro wasn't about to let that happen to his nest egg. He hadn't become an expert online shopper for nothing! So, he came up with a plan – to give generously but wisely to responsible people and groups. He was looking to see if his grandkids were responsible and charities were trustworthy. He didn't hesitate to follow up and discover where his donations truly ended up. A long weekend was coming, and the cookout at Junior's tiny house seemed to be the right time to start this conversation about wealth transfer.

Junior had naturally gravitated toward a wife who shared his financial values. He eventually married one of the other financial genius kids, and their wedding gifts reflected their unique priorities. Instead of fancy gadgets or overpriced kitchen appliances that would not fit into their tiny house anyway, they created a wedding registry built on common sense, including an option to support their Roth IRA or contribute to their honeymoon.

The smell of barbeque was in the air, and Pedro jumped right into the conversation. "I've been looking into the subject of generational transfer of wealth."

Junior responded, "Yeah, same here. My kids are going to have different challenges, but I'd like for them to grow up with common sense and retain some middle-class values. I should probably duplicate most of what I learned from you, as the key is transferring values more than just money. At the same time, many young people lack the family support we have, so we can come up with ways to make a difference in society."

Junior's good neighbor overheard a bit of their conversation and commented, "You aren't just beating the odds – you are rewriting the rules." Pedro and Junior chuckled at the thought.

Pedro watched with pride as Junior navigated adulthood. Junior didn't chase luxury cars or vacation homes. Instead, he and his wife embraced common sense. Pedro and Crystal remained involved, eager to help Junior and his kids avoid the traps that ensnare so many families. "It's not about what you can buy today," he'd tell Junior. "It's about what you can give tomorrow."

Pedro, who once feared Junior might fall into the 70% of heirs who squander their inheritance, was now at peace. Junior wasn't going to be part of that statistic. He had the mindset to beat the system – focus on behavior and incentives, avoid greed and laziness, and rely on expert advice for big decisions. Sure, they weren't billionaires, but they had something better: financial freedom and a sense of purpose.

A focus on incentives and behavior – instead of "learning" – leads to generational success

On the drive home, Pedro grinned as he thought about the future and his and Crystal's life choices. Maybe he and Junior weren't royalty, but they had become something far more valuable. Junior would continue the legacy, passing on not just money but the wisdom to manage it. In a world where so many lose their wealth by the third generation, Junior and his family would beat the system, and that was worth more than any title or massive fortune.

Who needed to be a billionaire when you could be the Genius Next Door?

Moral

Kids raised in wealthy families often display a mix of positive and negative traits influenced by their upbringing. Positively, they may exhibit confidence, strong networking skills, and an ability to easily navigate social and financial systems. Many develop leadership qualities and an entrepreneurial spirit due to exposure to business and investment opportunities. However, they can also struggle with entitlement, risk aversion, and a lack of financial discipline, as wealth cushions them from failure. Some may experience pressure to meet family expectations, and many grapple with maintaining or growing the family fortune in adulthood.

Evidence

Within the study of generational wealth transfer, the "third generation rule" is commonly discussed. Around 90% of wealthy families lose their wealth by the third generation, and about 70% of wealthy families lose their wealth by the next generation.[54]

To avoid this trend, grandparents can play an active role in their grandchildren's lives. Their involvement – through telling stories, modeling examples, emotional support, and perhaps financial gifts – positively influences the grandchildren's financial wisdom, behavior, and education.

Challenge

Instead of becoming billionaires and giving too much money to our kids, families at Financial HEIRs discuss generational questions about training young people to become HEIRS …

---

[54] See Generational Wealth: Why Do 70% of Families Lose Their Wealth in the 2nd Generation?, 2018.

Helpful and generous, Educated spenders, Investors with common sense, and Resilient workers.

Part of life is helping other families along the way toward this lifestyle. Instead of joining the 90% whose grandkids waste their inheritance, we can beat the system and rally together. Join other families who are interested in generational success.

Reflect

When would be a good time to talk with your family about Financial HEIRs?

How would an Alumni Inner Circle benefit youth today?

Genius Next Door

While it is still fresh in your mind, what are the ideas you had while reading this chapter?

Write down a couple of action items for this year ...

In the last chapter, Pedro and the family discuss Joy and dancing!

CHAPTER 24
Financial Health is 90% Psychological

Pedro had always believed that discipline and hard work were the keys to success, but one afternoon, he had a revelation while watching the movie Inside Out with the family. "So, Joy's the one who should be in charge of our brain, huh?" Pedro muttered, stroking his chin as the animated emotions jostled for control of the main character's brain.

Clark, sitting nearby, laughed. "You know, that movie's onto something. We've been focusing too much on numbers and not enough on fun! Joy is the real fuel. I read the other day that joy is the secret to emotional resilience,[55] and we experience peace after a spike of joy.

Pedro raised an eyebrow. "Turns out, it's less about counting dollars and more about keeping our heads straight!"

Crystal laughed, "I think we've been doing math on autopilot and forgetting the rest."

Clark leaned back in his chair, grinning. "You can't take numbers to the grave, but a life well-lived? Now, that's something worth investing in!" He winked. "Remember, it's not just about saving money – it's about saving your sanity, too!"

Junior sat at the table, only partially watching the movie, crunching numbers for the second time that month like his life depended on it. "Dad, if I save just 5% more, I can …"

Pedro interrupted, waving a hand. "Junior, you're missing the point. Financial health isn't about hoarding numbers like a squirrel with acorns."

"But money's security!" Junior protested.

---

[55] See Warner & Hinman, 2020, p. 13-21.

Pedro chuckled. "Reaching financial health is basically 90% psychological. Sometimes, the right decision is to *spend* it! Money is just a tool to enhance people's health. What good is a mountain of acorns if you never enjoy the feast?"

A family focused on financial health must overcome the temptation to overly emphasize money as a means of security

---

Junior paused, staring at his calculator. "So ... I should take my wife out on a nice date and go dancing?"

Crystal grinned. "Now you're getting it, Junior. Don't forget the flowers!"

Moral

Over time, Pedro and the entire family learned that financial health is 90% psychological and 10% math.

We make almost all our decisions based on innumerable variables, which may not even be logical or numbers-based. No matter our age, we make financial decisions that seem reasonable based on what we know at the time.

We navigate life with a sense of certainty, believing the choices we make fit the world as we understand it. Without that belief, getting through the day would feel overwhelming. Our decisions may evolve with more knowledge, but at each moment, they are grounded in our understanding, helping us function with purpose and confidence.[56]

---

[56] "We don't wander around blind and confused. We have to think the world we operate in makes sense based on what we happen to know. It'd be too hard to get out of bed in the morning if you felt otherwise" (Housel, 2020, p. 202).

As we choose to spend and save, we must keep sight of the big picture. And when we cannot afford the flowers, we should still stop and smell them.

Evidence

In 2018, the *Journal of Financial Counseling and Planning* reported that positive financial behaviors are associated with life satisfaction.[57] This suggests that while money itself doesn't directly bring joy, being financially healthy – managing money wisely, avoiding debt, and saving for the future – does contribute to pleasure and life satisfaction. Financial health provides stability, reduces stress, and opens up opportunities, which can lead to a greater sense of well-being.

Instead of chasing money, the focus should be on achieving financial health. In this lifestyle, joy becomes more attainable, not because we have more money, but because we have better control and peace of mind over our finances. It's a valuable lesson for us … and a legacy of joy we can pass on to future generations.

Challenge

Get started with your HEIRs. Our worst choice is to do nothing, feeding our tendencies toward laziness and feeling overwhelmed by the unorganized areas of our lives. "Getting started is more important than becoming an expert."[58]

Fintech is a fancy phrase describing how the personal finance industry has become more web-based, requires increased computer skills, and demands more 21st-century knowledge to navigate. "Future financial decisions will be more complicated due to fintech and the growing sophistication of the advertising business."[59] If we are behind the curve now, it will only get worse.

---

[57] "Research shows that among young adults, positive financial behaviors are associated with financial satisfaction and subsequently financial satisfaction is associated with life satisfaction (citing Xiao, Tang, & Shim, 2009)" (Szendrey & Fiala, 2018, p. 290).
[58] See Sethi, 2019, p. 8.
[59] See Ariely & Kreisler, 2018, p. 238.

So change now! Businesses and governments are becoming smarter each year in terms of how to persuade people toward the messages they present.[60]

In life, there is "good" or "bad" or "good enough." If you get started this year, that's good enough. Instead of feeling overwhelmed, you'll love the feeling of progress and hope.

---

[60] "In 2014, 136 countries had incorporated behavioral sciences in some aspects of public policy" (Thaler, 2015, p. 344).

Reflect

To maintain sanity, what time or day is best for you to focus on financial health?

Since financial health is primarily psychological, how do you plan to move forward with personal psychological obstacles?

While it is still fresh in your mind, what are the ideas you had while reading this chapter?

Genius Next Door

Write down an action item for this year ...

APPENDIX I
Welcome to Financial HEIRs

Welcome to Financial HEIRs International, where we help you develop a Generational, Generous, and Genius lifestyle!

Paul's dad was an expert on personal finance in the 1980s, helping numerous people with their financial affairs. In a home like this, Paul eventually learned to become a hard worker and knowledgeable in some basic financial principles.

In college, Paul decided to major in Finance, so his adventure with money seemed to expand into new horizons in college. Interestingly, anytime the subject of "personal finance" surfaced in college classes, the professor skimmed through the material since it was not as intellectually challenging as the other sections on corporate finance or entrepreneurial finance. Mission accomplished … he had graduated with a finance degree.

Paul's problem, as with most Americans, was that he did not have good financial *behavior*. While he was somewhat frugal coming out of college, he had no experience buying a house or a car. So, by age 25, he found himself in the wrong house with the wrong car. Those two decisions far outweighed his decent choices in smaller financial decisions.

So Paul spent the next 20 years getting on track with his own personal financial health. During those twenty years, he realized that personal psychology enormously influenced our financial behavior, along with pressures from society, family, or friends.

In 2020, during the beginning of COVID-19, his son was turning thirteen. What would he teach his son about manhood? Specifically, what should a young person learn about financial health? Paul's goal was to *inspire* him toward solid financial *behavior*. Then Paul had an epiphany … Why not have kids live off their investment interest? The idea was simple, but convincing somebody to live that lifestyle was a completely different matter.

This began an interesting study of the "psychology of money" to better understand how to become financially healthy as an adult and pass along a generational inheritance of financial health.

Instead of giving you 20th-century advice from textbooks and dry teaching principles (BORING!), we will tell you an inspiring story about someone who used psychology to their advantage and improved their financial health.

Financial HEIRs International exists to help inspire each person in the family to save $100,000 to live out their dreams! Saving $100,000 is simpler than you think! We bring a message of hope. Both you and your HEIRs will be surprised that your lifestyle may not have to radically shift from how you live now.

Together, we can inspire the next generation to live off their interest! Follow this ingenious path that kids LOVE as they are inspired to develop a strong work ethic, smart shopping skills, generosity, and an appreciation for investing. Generational, Generous, and Genius!

We encourage you to stop procrastinating. Watch the other short videos below, and create a free account today.

APPENDIX II
Everyday Ed

Once upon a time, in a faraway land known as America, an aspiring but amateur psychologist named Edward found himself new to this amazing country. As part of his journey to becoming a U.S. citizen, Edward studied American history diligently. Amid his studies, he noticed a fascinating pattern: every 80 years, the United States went through a massive cultural shift. First, there was the Declaration of Independence. Roughly 80 years later, the Civil War era brought freedom for the slaves. And about 80 years after that, in the 1930s, America emerged as a global superpower.

Edward, being the bold chap he was, figured that the 2020s would bring another seismic shift in American culture. "Eighty years... 2020s... What's the big change this time?" he mused, scratching his head while sipping on a cup of herbal tea, which he believed made him think better. Then it hit him like a ton of bricks: the culture of debt that America had been swimming in for the past 80 years would shift to a culture of saving money—by necessity!

Edward was particularly horrified when he learned about the national debt. The government had borrowed over $34 trillion! That's twelve zeros, folks. At a 3% loan rate, Edward calculated that this meant the government was paying over $1 trillion a year in interest alone. "One trillion!" Edward exclaimed, nearly spilling his tea. "That's more than most countries' entire budgets! The only other nations spending $1-4 trillion annually are China, Japan, Germany, and India. Yet, the USA spends a trillion each year just in interest!" he groaned, shaking his head in disbelief.

But it wasn't just the government that was in over its head with debt—the average American household owed around $100,000. At a 5% loan rate, Edward realized that paying $5,000 a year in interest meant many Americans missed out on a nice vacation every year. "Imagine all the trips to the beach, the amusement parks, and the good ol' road trips across the country they could have had!" he thought. Edward was convinced that it was high time for a change. "We need a revolution!" he declared to his pet goldfish, who didn't seem all that interested. "We need a culture of saving money instead of a culture of debt!"

Driven by this newfound mission, Edward dove into the research. He stumbled upon a Nobel Prize-winning idea that suggested a small psychological trick could encourage people to save more money. This trick was all about combating their natural tendency to spend. "Why doesn't everyone know about this?" Edward wondered. Actually, most people exposed to the idea had already implemented it, but Americans had no idea.

He also learned that financial health is interwoven with physical health, satisfaction with life, joy, emotional well-being, academic performance, and even a sense of leaving a lasting legacy. "Imagine a club where people share these values," he thought. "A club of like-minded individuals who are focused on financial health, an elite social network… of regular people!" he chuckled at the idea.

Edward began dreaming of meeting amazing people who shared these views on financial health. He wanted his kids to grow up with friends living the right way and even hoped they might find a date from the "right crowd." At this hypothetical club, Edward and his friends could even learn about how artificial intelligence was transforming their world, growing together through the next 50 years of societal change.

Edward's research led him to compare traditional financial advice with the latest research and 21st-century strategies for financial health. It was a no-brainer to him that upgrading to the latest advice made sense. He learned a significant truth: financial choices are 90% psychological, even though most people don't realize it. "Aha! This is it!" he shouted to his goldfish, who remained unimpressed. "It's simple to form a family plan that is Generational, Generous, and Genius."

He also discovered something startling: young people today make at least 20 choices before they turn 25 that eventually turn into Million Dollar Decisions. "Americans need to know how to train young people during these critical years," Edward mused. Along the way, he found and created some practical tools to launch himself toward financial health. He developed a list of achievable goals for anyone in their first year of getting financially organized – just one action item per month! "Even I can handle that," he thought. Edward also created an assessment quiz to help people with busy lifestyles find an investment strategy that fits their schedule and skill set. The tools list kept growing, and Edward knew he had to share them with his imaginary club.

After scouring the internet, Edward finally found what he was looking for: Financial HEIRs International (FHI). They have been conducting trials and doctoral-level research since 2020 to find the best tips on financial health, examining the psychology of money to design an inspirational path forward for people of all ages. They even had philanthropy options like the Blessing to Benefactor mentorship program, a college scholarship giveaway, and scholarships to cover FHI annual fees.

Then came the lightbulb moment. "Wait," Edward muttered, "I see my doctor every year, my dentist, even my auto mechanic... but I've never thought to meet with a financial consultant." He realized it made total sense to schedule an Annual Review of his financial health, just like he did for everything else. So, he signed up for an Annual Review with FHI.

At FHI, Edward discovered a goldmine of free resources. There were numerous free classes offered by government agencies and non-profits online. Plus, this club offered cutting-edge online classes on financial health at a competitive price. The classes were free if you bought a club membership with a bundle! They also had periodic surprise freebies designed to inspire financial health. "Edward realized it was useless to simply give away money to his kids or grandkids. "They need a lifestyle of financial health," he thought. "Teach them to fish; don't just give them all your fish!" He chuckled at his newfound wisdom. "Inspiring young people is not easy," he admitted. So he took that question to his newfound friends at the club, and they pointed him to the right classes at FHI.

Free money!" Edward chuckled, remembering an FHI slogan.

After watching the past 80 years of American history cultivate a culture of debt, Edward found a practical path toward financial health.

Moral

The moral of Edward's story is simple: financial health is quite achievable if you surround yourself with a good team. Whether you join the club or take some classes one at a time, you can leave a financial health legacy!

Evidence

"We should admit that we have limited time and energy for financial decisions."[61]

Challenge

Becoming a member is free—just create your free account to explore your options. FHI's innovative teachings will inspire you and your HEIRs toward financial health!

---

[61] See Ariely & Kreisler, 2018, p. 240.

Reflect

Are you willing to spend 99% of your time pursuing your life dreams and only 1% of your time on financial health?

If you spent 5 hours a month (1% of your waking hours monthly) on financial health, what is one achievable goal for the first month?

While it is still fresh in your mind, what are the ideas you had while reading this chapter?

Genius Next Door

Write down an action item for this year ...

APPENDIX III
Eduardo Magnifico

Eduardo Magnifico has been interacting with FHI for several years, so if you are curious about what to expect once you sign up to join FHI, then his story will be very helpful.

Meet Eduardo Magnifico, a man with an impressive name and an unremarkable understanding of personal finance. He wasn't reckless with his money—no, not like those who spend $8 on avocado toast every morning—but he wasn't exactly swimming in gold coins like Scrooge McDuck. He lived semi-comfortably, paid his bills, and dreamed of someday figuring out what "financial health" really meant.

One day, Eduardo heard about this intriguing group called Financial HEIRs International (FHI) and decided to check it out. The words "Generational, Generous, and Genius" caught his attention. "I could be all three of those," he thought, nodding to himself. "I am pretty genius when it comes to figuring out which leftovers are still safe to eat."

After watching three videos on the FHI website, Eduardo was hooked. They were short to the point, and unlike any finance lecture he'd sat through in school, these were actually… interesting. He liked the idea of creating a legacy of financial health for his kids, grandkids, and maybe even that one cousin who still owed him money from 1998. So, he created a free account and was ready to dive in.

First up was the Dream Again assessment, where Eduardo had to prioritize his dreams. This wasn't your typical bucket list—this was a finance-focused dream list. As he stared at the options, Eduardo thought, "Do I want to work at my dream job, even if it pays less? Or should I launch that hot dog stand I've been daydreaming about?" The choices were tough, but Eduardo loved the idea of being financially secure while pursuing his passion projects and having more free time for family and vacations. Plus, the thought of leaving a generational legacy made him feel like some kind of money-saving superhero.

The Dream Again assessment also made him reflect on generosity, free time, and legacy. Eduardo had always been generous when it came to picking up the tab for a friend (okay, maybe not *always*, but definitely once or twice), and he liked the idea of aligning his financial life with his values. "I'm going to be one of those cool uncles who leaves behind a legacy, not just a bunch of weird stuff in the attic," he thought, feeling inspired.

Suddenly, Eduardo had a golden revelation. Which of these two options made the most sense? 1) Save $1,000 a year, or 2) Hire a consultant at FHI for $300 a year to help him advance his career, gain some key tips, and still save $700 a year.

It wasn't hard to see the smarter choice. So he signed up for a consultation with FHI, where they provided him with another assessment called Pathway to Freedom. It sounded dramatic, but hey, who doesn't want financial freedom?

During the consultation, Eduardo and his FHI advisor dove into fresh ideas on budgeting, career assessment, and tackling personal obstacles. They didn't throw around intimidating numbers or ask him about obscure tax laws (thankfully, because Eduardo didn't know what 1099 was and wasn't planning on asking). Instead, they broke it down into baby steps, one achievable goal per month. "Even I can handle that!" Eduardo thought, grateful for a plan that didn't make him feel like he needed a PhD in finance.

After this initial consultation, Eduardo saw the value in FHI's approach. He bought a bundle that included consultations, free classes, and—perhaps most exciting for Eduardo—the chance to join the Alumni Inner Circle. Quarterly consultations became his preference during the first year as he got his finances in order and mapped out a plan to inspire his family. But after that, he found an Annual Review was all he needed to keep things on track. "It's like listening to your favorite playlist, but without the annoying ads and songs you always skip."

The bundle also included FHI's classes on financial health, which Eduardo loved because they were short and designed for people with full schedules (or his short attention span). Each class came with a story, a moral, and some evidence about how the moral is true. "It's like TED Talks but with more money-saving tips and fewer standing ovations," Eduardo mused. He even considered giving the Annual Review consultation as a holiday gift to his relatives, a gift that would keep on giving, unlike the itchy sweaters from Aunt Rita.

In Eduardo's opinion, perhaps the best part of the FHI package was his membership in the Alumni Inner Circle. Now, this wasn't just any social club—it was filled with people who shared Eduardo's new goal of financial health. The members exchanged tips, shared stories about how financial health had impacted their daily lives, and even started new friendships. The club offered interviews with experts, a quarterly newsletter, and discussions about how to use artificial intelligence to advance your career and hobbies. "These people are amazing," Eduardo thought. "It's like a secret club for people who want to be a financial genius!"

Eduardo also began to notice how much FHI gave away for free. Their staff had helped many people for no charge, handed out free materials, and even offered a college scholarship every year. During their classes on Digital Budgeting, Eduardo discovered FHI's mentorship program, Blessing to Benefactor, learning how to secure a benefactor and offer to mentor someone else. FHI was even working on a K-12 curriculum to inspire kids from all backgrounds toward financial health. "This is how we change the world!" Eduardo thought, shaking his head in admiration.

While reflecting on his chosen path, relatives were his potential HEIRs (FHI's fancy word for the next generation). Immediately, another valuable nugget popped into his head. Which option is better? 1) Give $1,000 a year to your HEIR for college expenses, or 2) Give $300 for an FHI consultation to set them on a path of financial health, plus $700 toward their college fund.

The answer was clear to Eduardo—why give money without guidance when you could do both and set them up for a brighter future? He knew what his choice would be. With a smile, he decided to spread the word about Financial HEIRs International and the path to financial freedom. After all, "My legacy is about to change!"

With FHI's guidance, Eduardo and his HEIRs were each on track to save up $100,000. That's right—Eduardo's kids were going to be multi-millionaires someday, meanwhile living off their investment interest while their peers were still figuring out how to balance a checkbook. He was proud of the legacy he was leaving behind, a legacy of financial health that was truly Generational, Generous, and Genius.

As for hiring a Certified Financial Planner (CFP), Eduardo wasn't in a rush. Most required a minimum of $100,000 or $200,000 to even set up a meeting, so he was content with his Annual Reviews for now. After all, these consultations were packed with valuable insights, and he felt more organized than ever before. Eduardo was sleeping better at night, knowing that his financial health was moving in the right direction, and the amount of time it took to maintain this lifestyle was surprisingly minimal.

Moral

Of all the clubs he could have joined—golf, chess, birdwatching, you name it—Eduardo Magnifico realized that Financial HEIRs International was truly worth his time. He wasn't just securing his family's financial future—he was enjoying every step of the process. And that, my friends, is the real hope he found by partnering with FHI.

In the end, Eduardo's legacy was no longer just a hope or a dream—it was becoming a reality. And he knew, without a doubt, that his life (and his bank account) were changing in a way that was Generational, Generous, and Genius.

Reflect

What dream of yours is motivating enough for you to consider making changes in your lifestyle to achieve that dream?

Would you rather pursue this dream on your own or with a team?

While it is still fresh in your mind, what are the ideas you had while reading this chapter?

Genius Next Door

Write down an action item for this year ...

Genius Next Door

Page Blank Intentionally

EPILOGUE

We hope you enjoyed these discoveries! One of my friends teared up when realizing how much this would mean for his kids and how much it would have changed his life.

Any family can benefit by using a few – or a ton – of the ideas at Financial HEIRs.

Want to Say Thanks?

If this book has been helpful, indeed **there are people you know who should read it!** They will probably join you in these intriguing discussions as you all watch families get on track. As for birthday and holiday gifts, who do you know that would benefit?

Another great way to say *thanks* is to steer your friends to our website at www.FinancialHEIRs.com, where you will find the classes, some of which are free!

About the Author

Dr. Paul T. Blake has worked in various industries, including the corporate world, non-profits, blue-collar entrepreneurs, education, ministry ... and personal finance. His undergraduate degree in finance was inspired by his father, who raised him to follow wise financial advice. Yet the results were mixed. After generations of his family following the conventional wisdom, Dr. Blake saw the need to tweak the mainstream financial advice to *inspire* people differently.

To discover more about the author, visit his website at www.PaulBlake.org.

To find true peace, you need to follow the Prince of Peace ... Jesus.

BIBLIOGRAPHY

Abramitzky, R., & Boustan, L. (2022, June 1). Why the Children of Immigrants are the Ones Getting ahead in America. *Time Magazine*. https://time.com/6182715/immigrants-children-us-mobility/

Adams, J. (1780, May 12). *Letter from John Adams to his Wife Abigail Adams*. Massachusetts Historical Society. https://www.masshist.org/digitaladams/archive/doc?id=L17800512jasecond

Ariely, D., & Kreisler, J. (2018). *Dollars and Sense: How We Misthink Money and How to Spend Smarter*. Harper.

Berti, A. E., & Bombi, A. S. (1988). *The Child's Construction of Economics* (G. Duveen, Trans.). Cambridge University Press.

Blue, R., & Blue, J. (1992). *Raising Money-Smart Kids*. Thomas Nelson.

Chart of the Week: China's Thrift, and What to Do About It. (2018). International Monetary Fund Blog. https://www.imf.org/en/Blogs/Articles/2018/02/26/chart-of-the-week-chinas-thrift-and-what-to-do-about-it

Chen, J. (2024). *Exchange-Traded Fund (ETF): How to Invest and What It Is*. Investopedia. https://www.investopedia.com/terms/e/etf.asp

Dixon, H. (2022, October 3). *The End of Cheap Money Reveals Global Debt Problem*. NASDAQ. https://www.nasdaq.com/articles/the-end-of-cheap-money-reveals-global-debt-problem

Flynn, J. (2023). *20+ Shocking American Savings Statistics [2023]: Average Personal Savings Accounts, Demographics, and Facts.* Zippia: The Career Expert. https://www.zippia.com/advice/american-savings-statistics/

Harwood, J. (2007). *Understanding Communication and Aging.* Sage Publications.

Hayes, A. (2024). *Certified Public Accountant: What the CPA Credential Means.* Investopedia. https://www.investopedia.com/terms/c/cpa.asp

He, L. (2023). *Chinese Savers Stashed Away $2.6 Trillion Last Year.* CNN. https://www.cnn.com/2023/02/07/economy/china-record-savings-revenge-spending-intl-hnk/index.html

Henney, M. (2024, June 7). *Nearly Two-Thirds of Middle-Class Americans Say They are Struggling Financially.* Fox Business. https://www.foxbusiness.com/economy/nearly-two-thirds-middle-class-americans-say-struggling-gasping-air

Herron, J. (2023). *A Troubling Share of Americans aren't Paying their Credit Cards in Full: Survey.* Yahoo Finance. https://finance.yahoo.com/news/a-troubling-share-of-americans-arent-paying-their-credit-cards-in-full-survey-200409041.html

Holden, K., Kalish, C., Scheinholtz, L., Dietrich, D., & Novak, B. (2009). Financial Literacy Programs Targeted on Pre-School Children: Development and Evaluation. *La Follette School of Public Affairs at the University of Wisconsin-Madison, 2009–009*, 1–25.

Housel, M. (2020). *The Psychology of Money: Timeless Lessons on Wealth, Greed, and Happiness.* Harriman House.

Hyatt, M. (2024). *5 Research-Backed Benefits of Making Generosity a Habit*. Full Focus. https://fullfocus.co/habit-of-generosity/

IsHak, W. W. (Ed.). (2020). *The Handbook of Wellness Medicine*. Cambridge University Press. https://www.cambridge.org/core/books/abs/handbook-of-wellness-medicine/sleep-rest-and-relaxation-in-improving-wellness/FD5079A99C835009BB5EA2AC0CE53591

Jorgensen, B. L., Allsop, D. B., Runyan, S. D., Wheeler, B. E., Evans, D. A., & Marks, L. D. (2019). Forming financial vision: How Parents Prepare Young Adults for Financial Success. *Journal of Family and Economic Issues, 40*, 553–563.

Kagan, J. (2023). *Certified Financial Planner (CFP): What It Is and How to Become One*. Investopedia. https://www.investopedia.com/terms/c/cfp.asp

Kersting, K. (2004). Brain Research Advances Help Elucidate Teen Behavior. *American Psychological Association, 35*, 80.

Kiyosaki, R., & Lechter, S. (2001). *Rich Dad's Rich Kid Smart Kid: Giving Your Child a Financial Head Start*. Warner Business.

Konish, L. (2024). *Most of Warren Buffett's Wealth was Accumulated after Age 65. Here's what that can Teach Individual Investors*. CNBC. https://www.cnbc.com/2024/05/03/most-of-warren-buffetts-wealth-came-after-age-65-heres-why.html

LeBaron, A. B., Hill, E. J., Rosa, C. M., Spencer, T. J., Marks, L. D., & Powell, J. T. (2018). I Wish: Multigenerational Regrets and Reflections on Teaching Children about Money. *Journal of Family and Economic Issues, 39*, 220–232.

LeBaron, A. B., Rosa-Holyoak, C. M., Bryce, L. A., Hill, E. J., & Marks, L. D. (2018). Teaching Children about Money: Prospective Parenting Ideas from Undergraduate Students. *Journal of Financial Counseling and Planning*, *29*(2), 259–271.

Losch, D. (2020). *Giving Outside the Box*. Self-published.

Matthews, M. (2014). *We've Crossed the Tipping Point: Most Americans Now Receive Government Benefits*. Forbes. https://www.forbes.com/sites/merrillmatthews/2014/07/02/weve-crossed-the-tipping-point-most-americans-now-receive-government-benefits/

Generational Wealth: Why do 70% of Families Lose Their Wealth in the 2nd Generation? (2018). NASDAQ. https://www.nasdaq.com/articles/generational-wealth:-why-do-70-of-families-lose-their-wealth-in-the-2nd-generation-2018-10

National Center for Health Statistics. (2019). *Life Expectancy at Birth, age 65, and age 75, by Sex, Race, and Hispanic Origin: United States, Selected Years 1900–2019*. Center for Disease Control and Prevention. https://www.cdc.gov/nchs/data/hus/2020-2021/LExpMort.pdf

Once-in-a-Generation Wealth Boom Ends for America's Middle Class. (2023). Bloomberg. https://www.bloomberg.com/graphics/2022-us-midterms-middle-class-wealth/?leadSource=uverify%20wall

Orman, S. (2005). *The Money Book for the Young, Fabulous, and Broke*. Riverhead Books.

Owen, D. (2007). *The First National Bank of Dad: The Best Way to Teach Kids about Money*. Simon & Schuster.

Parker, T. (2024). *How Much Does It Cost to Raise a Child in the U.S.?* Investopedia. https://www.investopedia.com/articles/personal-finance/090415/cost-raising-child-america.asp

Priday, B. (2020). *Are Rich People Really Less Generous?* Econofact. https://econofact.org/are-rich-people-really-less-generous

Ramsey, D., & Cruze, R. (2014). *Smart Money Smart Kids: Raising the Next Generation to Win with Money.* Lampo Press.

Sabri, M. F., Gudmunson, C. G., Griesdorn, T. S., & Dean, L. R. (2020). Influence of Family Financial Socialization on Academic Success in College. *Journal of Financial Counseling and Planning, 31*(2), 267–283.

Sethi, R. (2019). *I Will Teach You to be Rich.* Workman Publishing.

Spuhler, B. K., & Dew, J. (2019). Sound Financial Management and Happiness: Economic Pressure and Relationship Satisfaction as Mediators. *Journal of Financial Counseling and Planning, 30*(2), 157–174.

Stanley, T. J., & Danko, W. D. (2010). *The Millionaire Next Door: The Surprising Secrets of America's Wealthy.* Taylor Trade Publishing.

Sun, S., & Chun, Y.-C. (2022). Is Financial Capability a Determinant of Health? Theory and Evidence. *Journal of Family and Economic Issues, 43*, 744–755.

Szendrey, J., & Fiala, L. (2018). "I think I can get ahead!" Perceived Economic Mobility, Income, and Financial Behaviors of Young Adults. *Journal of Financial Counseling and Planning, 29*(2), 290–303.

Taylor, M. (2022). *Money Patterns Are Set by Age 7 – Here's What You Should and Should Not Be Teaching Your Kids*. Parents.com. https://www.parents.com/parenting/better-parenting/advice/money-patterns-are-set-by-age-7-heres-what-you-should-and-should-not-be-teaching-your-kids/

Tenney, J., Kalenkoski, C. M., Serido, J., & Shim, S. (2021). Where Knowledge Meets Perceptions: Emerging Adults and their Perceptions of Financial Knowledge. *Journal of Personal Finance, 20*(2), 89–102.

Thaler, R. H. (2015). *Misbehaving: The Making of Behavioral Economics*. WW Norton & Company.

Twenge, J. M. (2017). *iGen: Why Today's Super-Connected Kids Are Growing Up Less Rebellious, More Tolerant, Less Happy—And Completely Unprepared for Adulthood—And What That Means for the Rest of Us*. Atria Books.

Warner, M., & Hinman, S. (2020). *Building Bounce: How to Grow Emotional Resilience*. Deeper Walk International.

Weinschenk, S. (2013). *Use Unpredictable Rewards to Keep Behavior Going*. Psychology Today. https://www.psychologytoday.com/au/blog/brain-wise/201311/use-unpredictable-rewards-to-keep-behavior-going

Whitebread, D., & Bingham, S. (2013). *Habit Formation and Learning in Young Children*. The Money Advice Service. https://mascdn.azureedge.net/cms/the-money-advice-service-habit-formation-and-learning-in-young-children-may2013.pdf

Wolfe, R. (2024, August 28). The American Dream Feels Out of Reach for Most. *Wall Street Journal*. https://archive.is/Gtl7T

Worthington, A. K., Nussbaum, J. F., & Bergstrom, M. J. (2018). *Intergenerational Communication*. Oxford Bibliographies. https://www.oxfordbibliographies.com/display/document/obo-9780199756841/obo-9780199756841-0217.xml